White Feather Press

Reaffirming Faith in God, Family, and Country!

CONTENTS

America

BAAL'd

Out

Results of the Powerless Gospel in
the Lawless Churches

Pastor Wayne North

Acknowledgements and Thanks

I would like to thank the Father, Son and Holy Spirit for their expression of love and purpose that they have saturated upon me. My wife, Kristine, for her relentless love for God and her inspirational life that she demonstrates every day. My daughter Brooke, Hunter and Kansas for loving the Lord and putting up with my "rants." My church family that supplements my life within their callings and spiritual gifts. The 'flavor' of person God has designed me to be is because of all of you who have poured into me the ingredients of God's character and love that He designed you to be. I want to encourage all of you to seek first His Kingdom and His righteousness, and He will add to your life everything you nccd for a succcssful eternity.

Introduction

As we see dozens of churches close their doors each day, we must ask ourselves "Why?" As we see tens of thousands of people walk through the doors of mega-churches only to remain the same as they were before they came to Christ, we also must also ask ourselves "Why?" As we are only evangelizing less than 4 percent of the population, we must ask ourselves "Why?" As we see a culture with a 1 percent biblical worldview, we know the church is dying. In fact, many churches with thousands of members are dead spiritually. They just have great programs.

In the Western church, we do not rely upon God, especially the Holy Spirit, for sustenance and viability. Our society has become self-centered and entertainment driven, including our churches. We have killed transformations in favor of information. We have settled for numbers rather than truths. We have focused on the needs of people and their favor rather than pleasing God and seeking His favor.

We cannot earn His love or salvation. But Scripture states that He desires obedience (Luke 11:28). We can earn His favor and promotion. While many may argue with me, I really don't care. God's eyes search across the earth for righteous hearts and lives. So while many people are asking "Why?"; while many are playing weekly church either in small churches or megachurches; while many believe God did away with His precepts and laws; while many believe God is okay with sinful lives; while many can't believe how fast sin and perversity are consuming are society; while most are observing the prevalence of darkness overtaking the earth and how days are getting worse, I have decided, rather than focusing only on the whys, we should be walking out our faith by exclaiming "Why Not?!" That has become the series title. It was given to my wife through the inspiration of the Holy Spirit.

While we are told not to be troubled (John 14:8), these things must happen. We continue to run the race. If we believe Christ is who he said He is and the Holy Spirit will do what He says He will do, we will press on and be empowered to do even greater things than Christ—not because of us but because of the One who lives inside us. The same Spirit who raised Christ from the dead and empowered Jesus to do the will of the Father has empowered us to follow in His footsteps and the disciples, and their disciples. So Why Not?!

Why Not ... Live a holy life?

Why Not ... Believe in miracles?

Why Not ... Prepare people for the next step?

Why Not ... Be countercultural?

Why Not ... Be real and relevant?

Why Not ... Present the only truth?

Why Not ... Raise the greatest godly generation ever?

Why Not ... Be bold?

Why Not?! ... Why Not?! ... Why Not?!

Dedication

I dedicate this and all my success to God, and those He has placed in my life that challenge, encourage and refine me to be able to do far more than I could ever dream or imagine through Christ's power and kingdom principles.

Be Worshipful,

Become His Story!

Why Not?!

Chapter 1

Worship

WHAT DO YOU WORSHIP? Better yet, what is worship? Is it music? Is it a slow song? Maybe it's raising your hands. Maybe it's sitting solemnly. Maybe it's_____. You fill in your definition. Merriam-Webster defines worship this way:

- to honor or reverence as a divine being or supernatural power
- to regard with great or extravagant respect, honor, or devotion
- to perform or take part in worship or an act of worship

Worship could be of God or anything we place highly in our lives. I feel that, as believers, we are in sin when we disobey God or not do what God says. Even more, we are in sin when we preach any other Jesus than who He really was and is! We have even idolized the "Jesus" we have made up in our heads. The new "Jesus" that is being worship is a different Jesus being preached. He even gave up His life to be obedient to His Father as an example to us of what we should be doing. Lukewarm Christians are those who are neither hot nor cold. They look like the world while proclaiming to be believers. In essence, they have two masters. Scripture states:

> *Do not lay up treasures on earth*
> *for yourselves, where moth and rust*
> *corrupt, and where thieves break*
> *through and steal. But lay up treasures*
> *in Heaven for yourselves, where neither*
> *moth nor rust corrupt, and where thieves*
> *do not break through nor steal. For*
> *where your treasure is, there will your*
> *heart be also. The light of the body is*
> *the eye. Therefore, if your eye is sound,*
> *your whole body shall be full of light.*
> *But if your eye is evil, your whole body*
> *shall be full of darkness. If therefore*
> *the light that is in you is darkness, how*
> *great is that darkness! No one can serve*
> *two masters. For either he will hate the*
> *one and love the other, or else he will*
> *hold to the one and despise the other.*
> *You cannot serve God and mammon.*

> *Therefore, I say to you, do not be
> anxious for your life, what you shall eat,
> or what you shall drink; nor for your
> body, what you shall put on. Is not life
> more than food, and the body more than
> clothing?*
>
> *(Matthew 6:19-25)*

We see a church that wants to both love the world and be able to go heaven. I am hesitant about saying the word "Jesus" in the previous paragraph. If we love Jesus, we will obey His commandments (John 14:15). We love our masters by obeying them. A sign of love is obedience. Children are commanded to obey their parents and then they will live long lives (a promise). Obedience is an act of worship much deeper than a song or church action we do once a week. Obedience is related to submission. Wives are to submit to their husbands in honor. Christ served the church as husbands are to serve their wives in honor. Other Scriptures state:

> *Jesus knew their thoughts and said to
> them, every kingdom divided against
> itself is brought to desolation. And every
> city or house divided against itself shall
> not stand.*
>
> *(Matthew 12:25)*

> *If a house is divided against itself, that house cannot stand.*
>
> *(Mark 3:25)*

Is it possible that the reason why there is so much despair and devastation in the world, and even in the church, is because we aren't sold out for Him? Is it because we are trying to serve two masters? We are trying to look like the world because we want its approval. We don't like being persecuted or even looking different. We think we will be miserable. No! We are miserable as we try to serve two masters. I believe the Matthew Scriptures referred to earlier tie together the connection between serving two masters and the door being left open for anxiousness to enter our lives. I have never seen a person who is chasing after Christ be controlled by fear or anxiety. I have seen people get sidetracked from the race set before them by Christ and become anxious or fearful. Everything we have in this world, beyond the spiritual ingredients, will rust, break down, decay, die, leave or …

When we don't worship Him in spirit and in truth, we become dull and insensitive to His calling and voice. We lack relationship and intimacy with Him. And since there is no vacuum in the spiritual realm, as our distance increases between the Lord and us, the enemy moves in and begins running interference.

But God requires us to worship Him in spirit and in

truth. Not in our body! Not in our mind! True worship results from the overflow from the Spirit. But many fleshly, carnal Christians rely upon their feelings and moods to determine their worship.

As we begin to worship Him in every action of every day, because we focus on Him, we will be in a constant state of worship. Most Christians worship periodically throughout the week. Many only do it in song or bodily movement at the worship service they attend occasionally during the month. What a sad expression of love we have for Him! We are in love with ourselves more than we are with Him. Point blank: We love ourselves more than Him! We are to die to our own desires. We are to love what He loves and hate what He hates. Do you? Or do you disregard His character and Word because it makes you uncomfortable? Do you love the sin of this world more than the sinner who will go to hell unless they repent and turn away from their wicked ways?

You must remember that perfect people don't go to heaven; forgiven people go to heaven. Forgiveness can occur only through humility. Humility occurs when we realize that we deserve hell. God, being righteous, has the right and obligation to His character to separate sin from His holiness. We have no right to determine what is holy and what is not. That is why we are commanded to judge according to His righteousness. All compliments and criticisms are judgment calls. We are commanded to base our judgments upon the Holy

Scriptures and His righteousness. Humility stems from submission and utter dependence upon His grace to not only save us from hell and its torment, but also the power to change us into His image. We are called to follow in His footsteps. As He could only do what His Father was doing, so should we (John 5:19). Jesus also states:

> *I can do nothing of My own self. As I hear, I judge, and My judgment is just, because I do not seek My own will, but the will of the Father who has sent Me.*
>
> *(John 5:30)*

If we are to judge righteously, we need to follow His will, which we find outlined in Scripture. I say outlined because God is not 100 percent explained in Scripture. His identity and nature are encapsulated within it. Scripture places the boundaries of our faith much like a person putting a puzzle together first does the edges. If we do not know the "edges" of Scripture, we will not be able to be fill in our faith picture. I believe God still speaks to His children through dreams and visions, audibly, through signs and wonders, through other people, and so on. There is no new revelation, but there is fresh revelation as He reveals more of Himself to us. As we surrender more of our lives, God fills the "me" spot with Himself. The baptism of the Holy Spirit is nothing more than a deeper filling of the Holy Spirit by emptying ourselves to be full of Him. Although all of us receive the Holy Spirit in our new birth in Christ, we aren't always at equal points in the filling process.

Jesus stated that, if He didn't do His Father's will, then people shouldn't believe in Him (John 10:37-38). Maybe the hypocrisy in the church would cease if we would do the same. Maybe we should say the same: "If I don't do what Jesus did and said, then don't follow me." The world has already quit following the church because we aren't following the Holy Spirit who reveals the truth of Jesus Christ. When we are spirit led, and follow the truth, then we are in worship. Jesus stated:

> *Truly, truly, I say to you, He who believes on Me, the works that I do he shall do also, and greater works than these he shall do, because I go to My Father. And whatever you may ask in My name, that I will do, so that the Father may be glorified in the Son.*
>
> *(John 14:12–13)*

When we believe in Him and are "in" Him, we are truly worshipping. I don't understand the greater works totally. But I do know that we, through His power and authority, will be His ambassadors in this world and carry His mantle, this same mantle. We will do all the examples He set for us as "Christ"-ians, and new ones that will proclaim Him in our culture. His truth has not changed, but its application in a twenty-first-century world will look slightly different. The same Holy Spirit (who allowed Jesus to overcome the world and express the kingdom principles through healing, miracles, signs, and wonders) will work through you too! I believe these signs will follow those who believe. True believers should manifest His presence just because they bathe in it. This is true worship.

I had the opportunity to console a young man who was told he was done playing football because he had probably torn his ACL, MCL, and possibly more tissue in his knee. I could see he was in conflict and overcome with grief and despair. It hurt me to see him in such a disarray. As I walked away, I simply turned around and said I would be praying for a miracle. In his atheistic reaction, he escaped beyond my words into some hopeless and meaningless jargon. Yet, Monday of the following week, he met me at the door. He told me that the doctors had recanted on their diagnosis. They couldn't see the damage anymore. All they could see was a bruise on the MRI that previously revealed the tears. Coincidence? I think not! More of a "God-incidence"! I looked at him and said that must be the miracle I prayed for. He just stared at me. God had revealed Himself to a young man who had been damaged by religious traditions that probably had hurt and maimed him. It was just that simple. I asked, He showed up, His answer followed!

We hunger and thirst after righteousness. We seek Him with all our hearts and we do find Him. When we are in Christ, He gets glorified and so does the Father. When we deny these things, we deny Him the opportunity to glorify His Father. We glorify Jesus, who glorifies the Father. Again, this is true worship. Don't seek after a worship experience. Seek after Him! Then you will experience true worship—24/7 worship!

So why haven't you walked in this type of faith? You are probably too full of yourself or the ways of the world to leave room for of God. You want more? Then surrender more, and more, and more!

> *Whatever you do in word or deed, do*
> *all in the name of the Lord Jesus, giving*
> *thanks to God and the Father by Him.*
>
> *(Colossians 3.17)*

The above verse, to me, explains our purpose in life. When we take every thought captive to the knowledge and truth of Jesus Christ, we will do what is right. When we put our minds on things above and not things below (of the world), we will do His will. We will find His will when we dwell upon:

*Whatever things are true, whatever
things are honest, whatever things
are right, whatever things are pure,
whatever things are lovely, whatever
things are of good report; if there is any
virtue and if there is any praise, think on
these things.*

(Philippians 4:8)

Is it these things we dwell upon? No! If we dwell upon God who *is* these things, we will lead a life of worship! We are commanded to be in this world, but not of it. We are commanded not to be conformed to this world, but be transformed by the renewing (washing) of our lives (Romans 12:2). He predestined us to be in the image of Christ through His power (Romans 8:29).

So why haven't you walked in this level of worship?

Be Worshipful, Become His Story!

Why Not?!

Pastor Wayne North

Be His Story, Become Transformed!

Why Not?!

Chapter 2

My Story

I WAS RAISED IN A CHURCH-GOING family. We were Sabbath keepers. Yeah, I can hear your judgment about me now. "He must be legalistic and trying to earn his way into heaven." "Those Sabbath keepers look down upon the rest of us." "Don't they know that the law was done away with by Jesus?" And so on. Before you get your royal loin cloth in a bundle, hear what I have to say.

I went to church weekly. I accepted Jesus Christ at an early age, around four to six years. On the farm, I remember taking any animal that died out to a designated spot, where I met with God and prayed that, in all His power, if it be His will, in the name of Jesus, He would bring that animal back to life. And then, I buried them. No, not one of them ever came back to life! Yet, in my childlike faith, I knew He could do it.

As I grew, I grew in knowledge and wisdom—*of the world*! I started to skip church only for special occasions. Then, I began to think that everything was the special occasion: hunting, fishing, sports, TV, tiredness, and so on. My heart toward God began to grow cold. I never quit believing in Him; I quit worshipping Him. I knew He was love. I forgot He was righteous and deserving!

This continued throughout my high school years and beyond. In fact, when I received the calling of pastor later in life, I think my former pastors from my teens shed a few tears of unbelief. They had almost written me off as I went off to college to chase after the world. But, like most in the church who profess to be Christians, I did much of what everyone else did. Believe me, I didn't do the sinful stuff like drugs and murder. I only drank and got drunk. I had a rebellious heart that would lead me to swear and push the line. Yet, I would still ask forgiveness in the end. Sound familiar?

I married my high school sweetheart after eight years of her putting up with me. She would be having Bible study in her dorm room while I would be out partying or trying to break the reportedly "unbreakable" glass windows of the library windows. My friends and I actually found out they were breakable. She would be doing the right thing and I would do the worldly thing.

After we got married and settled in, we were invited to a Bible study with our neighbors on Friday nights.

Friday nights were football games. A good, loving God wouldn't hold it against me if I didn't go. After all, I asked for forgiveness and prayed sometimes. I knew Him as my Savior. But I didn't know Him as Lord.

We finally went, after we told our hosts that I had to leave to see the second half of the game. It was a loving gesture to watch those players. Isn't it good to be loving? Poor excuse!

As I watched God reveal Himself through answered prayers, deliverance, healing, and other signs and wonders, I started to understand that there was more to this whole thing. The words of Scripture began to jump off the page and become real. I began to experience God through His truth. I saw marriages healed. I heard tongues and interpretation being used. I observed demonized people being set free. I witnessed the sick being made well. I felt and experienced worship too. I started to see God in a new and deeper way.

In 1992, my wife began to work with youth in our community. Each week we would invite youth to our house for study, food, and fun. Each week, she would bring the study and food. I brought the fun! I was her sidekick. Kind of like Abbott and Costello, Martin and Lewis, ice cream and toppings … well maybe not quite. Yet, you get my depth and importance in the mix. I was seeing God move and it was exciting. But I was still a spectator and not a participant. Then after a few years, we had an open question night at the church. One girl asked if could we drink alcohol and still be a Christian.

As one of the leaders, I jumped right up and answered very … worldly. I told her God didn't have a problem with drinking; just don't become a drunkard. Sounds good, right? This had been my experience. Getting drunk only a few times in a week doesn't make you a drunkard!

I was *so* proud of myself. On the way home, I glowed with my newfound wisdom. For the first time in recent years, I heard my heavenly Father say, "How dare you speak on my behalf about something for which you do not have My truth or heart!" Ouch! Did He just do that? For the next week I struggled with this rebuke and redirection. I knew I had to apologize for being carnal and unbiblical. It was hard and humbling. But very rewarding and restoring.

Not too long after that, I began counseling youth. Many of the youth in our area are from families with symptoms of alcoholism and drug abuse prevalent within their homes. I was doing my best in my untransformed life to give them Jesus, but the power wasn't there.

Then during our community's annual festivities, I was having a beer (not drunk, just being social). One boy I worked with walked by and gave me the saddest look ever. In his mind, I was just like his parents. He couldn't distinguish between my choices and his parent's choices. I just became part of the problem. I never had the opportunity to speak into this child's life again.

At this point, I studied the Scripture and decided I

was going to quit drinking alcohol. I have since then made it a requirement for all my leaders too. I am not going to be the alcohol police and see if they drank wine or cooked with it. I will deal with it when it becomes a public statement.

I always drank to get a "buzz" on. And from my study of Scripture, the "buzz" is a word for being drunk. Besides that, I believe all leaders should beyond reproach. We aren't to ask the question, "What can I do and still be saved?" We should be asking, "What do I get to do now that I am saved?" These two questions clearly identify the focus of the statement. The first is from the world and the sin nature. The second is focused on His nature and His kingdom's principles.

The next thing I heard was God's voice to give up all secular music. What? First He asked me to give up my drinking and the drinking buddies who went with that. And now my "precious" (think Lord of the Rings) music.

I had a childhood dream of being the lead singer of a rock band. God revealed to me that to go where He wanted for me to go would take sacrifice and holiness. If I wanted to do what Jesus did, I would have to live like Jesus did through His amazing grace. My car radio has been set to Christian stations ever since.

He began to open up opportunities immediately. It wasn't even hard! Yeah, I do hear some of my old favorites when at stores or gas stations. I can remember every word, or at least what I thought were the words.

I realized that music is powerful. Maybe it's true that Lucifer was in charge of worship music in heaven. Maybe that is why we don't see many references to music in heaven in Scripture after his expulsion! It was after this that I began to be a participant in God's miraculous, powerful grace.

I began writing articles in monthly publications, directing camps and retreats, to be asked to speak at conferences, and more. I got to see the process of sanctification being played out in my life. The more I gave up, the more I received. I began to reap blessings because I sowed blessings. I started to work in new spiritual gifts, and see the gifts God placed on others. I began working in deliverance ministry wherever I would go. I could see the bondages people were in, as I was once in them too. God began to show me not just the don'ts of life but the consequences He was trying to save His children from experiencing. It was exciting but also a burden because of the lack of desire to "be holy because He *is* holy."

I started to see the covenants we make with the world around us. I could see the covenants I made with music and pain in my life. We can't be in two covenants opposing one another—one of death and despair, the other leading to life, and more abundant life. No wonder people are miserable. No wonder so many Christians are miserable! They have made covenants with their pain and past. Coming to Jesus doesn't clean you up. It erases the consequences of eternal life. There is still the process of sanctification that God wants to do so that you can be a witness of His goodness, mercy, and grace to those in this world. He did not save you to have a personal experience. He saved you to tell the world. This is why evangelism is so hard for the American church. Most people look at it as only a change in your destination after you leave this location. Scripture says He has placed eternity in the hearts of men (now), and we are to be living sacrifices—ambassadors into this world with His seal upon us.

During that time, I experienced His power and truth firsthand. I no longer fought with His goodness. Now I no longer question His character from Genesis 1 through the end of Revelation. All of it is His redemptive story for me. I am not a New Testament believer. I am a Full Testament believer. Everything was written for me to glean and apply to my DNA. I am burdened when people start making the Bible with holes, rather than keeping it holy!

It was here that signs and wonders began to follow me because I followed Him! I now expect Him to show up. I don't need to argue people into the kingdom. I just allow Him to be released like He did with the woman at the well, the lame, the sick, the blind, the lepers, woman with the blood issue, the mad man, the demonized, and many others. I will lift His name high so that He may draw all men to Himself.

Evangelism is easy once you have tasted the Word and its power. You will not be able to contain it. We overcome the enemy by the blood of Jesus and word of our testimony, even to death. We must die so we can overcome—die to our shame, guilt, condemnation, desires, pride, and whatever else is stopping us from being His witnesses. I experienced His kingdom and now I can't help but share it.

At the first retreat I ever directed; God challenged me. I had my plans. I was going to teach on spiritual warfare. This is part of His calling on my life and I was going to share my knowledge. I got to the camp a day ahead to work on the responsible things of preparing packets and handouts. After about ten hours of work and copying, I had multiple stacks of hundreds of papers. I was so proud! I sat back just in time for the Lord to say "good job but I have something else in mind." What! And then He showed up.

As people showed up, there was sickness upon many of them. They all wanted prayer. I had less than ten hours of sleep in five days. Every night we had spiritual counseling, healing, and deliverance. It wasn't until the last night that God revealed His power in its fullness for all to see. Before that night individuals experienced His healing grace. The last night everyone got to experience it firsthand, including myself. Now it's been over 25 years later, and I have participated in thousands of salvations, deliverances, healings, miracles, signs and wonders. Some of these encounters are still too strange for me to talk about here. Yet every time, the power of the Gospel was real and relational.

Are you ready for God to *rock* your world? Again, remember that as a young child, I used to take our dead animals and ask God to restore their lives. Never once did any of them came back to life. Then I would bury them. I was never taught to do this. I just remember reading about my Daddy in Scripture and the power He released into His Son through the Holy Spirit to do such things. My childlike faith believed what He said about who He was and is!

It's time to re-enact our childlike faith. We have tried to run the church for too long. We have fine-tuned programs, professional worship teams, and trained teachers and pastors. Yet we lack His power and vision. We see thousands accepting Christ as their Savior and being baptized, only to see tens of thousands walk out of the church with the same issues they walked in with. Jesus didn't suffer, die, and rise from the dead so I can sin more, or even remain in my sin. We are mocking Him by our sinful desires and lifestyles and a lack of transformational gospel power.

So why aren't we seeing more miracles, and signs and wonders as He promised?

Be His Story, Become Transformed!

Why Not?!

Be Transformed,

Become Obedient!

Why Not?!

Chapter 3

From Caterpillar to Butterfly

ONE TIME MY MENTORING PAStor, Dale Smalley, told my wife and me about some spiritual experiences he was encountering in the ministry. Dale is the pinnacle of what I would label as a spiritual man. He would wake sometimes up to two hours before work to read, study, and pray each morning. He encouraged everyone to read the Bible through each year from cover to cover. He believed every word it says. The stories he told sounded like they came right off the pages of Scripture. We didn't doubt him one bit. Yet, when he was done, my wife spoke for both of us: "That may be good for you, but that's not for us!" She also added, "You're crazy." He received it well and just reiterated that, if we continued to grow and remain in ministry long enough, we would see signs and wonders follow our activated and growing faith.

A transitional moment for me was watching Dale deliver a young lady who came to that Bible study I mentioned earlier. Green vomit emitted from her as Dale proclaimed Jesus's name over her and trampled upon the demons that held her in bondage. As these demons left, her face shone brighter and brighter. If you've never encountered deliverance, then you really haven't seen God's true defeat of the devil and his cohorts.

Much of what we see Jesus do in Scripture deals with demons. I feel one third of His ministry was trampling upon their territory as He stormed the gates of Hades and set the captives free. Then He commanded His disciples to do the same. He commanded them to teach all He taught them. Then, He said, greater things we shall do than He did because we are many with the same Holy Spirit that empowered Him living inside of us. Praise God! This is an example of the power of the gospel we should expect to see and experience in His church.

We see people make decisions and accepting Jesus in the church. Yet, they stay tormented and addicted to sin issues. They never find peace. They hear about this grace and mercy we've been given. Yet, because the church doesn't understand it, we can't teach it to others, let alone allow others to experience it. We have simplified grace into the "big cover-up." We teach that

Jesus has forgiven everyone's sin. We teach it is a free gift. We teach that we don't have to do anything to receive it. All of these are partially true. Partial truths are also partial lies. Lies lead us into bondages. No wonder most who make commitments return to their old ways.

How dare we simplify God's grace into less than it really is! God's grace empowers us to live out what Scripture commands us to do. Mercy allows us not to get what we deserve. Grace allows us receive what we don't deserve. God doesn't need us; He wants us. This is a higher form of love. He could do it all by Himself. Yet He chooses to work though His people and His church. He is sovereign. He can do whatever He wants on His own. He can choose to use whomever He wants to accomplish His will.

It was huge revelation to me that He doesn't need me; He wants me! In His sovereignty, He designed me with free will. He allows my choices to affect His working. I don't get it, but I know it works. Obedience opens the door of blessing and working in my life. I believe God's promises are conditional. There are guidelines and instructions for us to follow. Disobedience may even cause destruction rather than blessing.

I wonder when I hear people or churches refer to themselves as "New Testament" followers. Basically, they seem to be saying they are free from the what they consider to be misguided rules the Father set up before Jesus came. They imply that, like our earthly fathers, God the Father had a little bit of an anger issue and set up some really outrageous laws to follow. Thank God (the Son) for coming to set things straight. During the process the Father must have got some anger management classes and now He is love! Hogwash! He hasn't changed. When the disciples were referring to Scripture, it was literally the Old Testament that brought truth and that Truth was Jesus Christ. Until we become the "Whole Testament" church we will continue to see sin control the church and transformation cease to exist at any relevant level. Thus, only a form of godliness will exist, with little power.

I recently explained it to a man who trying to explain to me that the law was done away with and now we live by relationship. I agree with that, but obedience is an act of our relationship. We now are living in about the fourth decade of the "twisted" grace movement. I explained to him that I didn't know he was such a hypocrite. I kidded around that I used to look up to him, but now I was devastated! He looked at me very puzzled and asked why I considered him a hypocrite. Well, wasn't it obvious? If God did away with the law, then with what right did he have to enforce house rules for his children like curfews, cleaning their rooms, and the like. He just nodded and said, "You got me!" I am a firm believer that God will love even those who will be eternally in hell. Obedience brings spiritual promotion. Disobedience brings in open attack from the enemy. God's universe is set up by physical and spiritual laws because He is a God of order. The rules (laws) were created because of who He is!

David was totally forgiven for his Bathsheba sin. But it allowed sin to enter into his household. We see the destruction carry through his family line (generational curse). Although generational curses can be broken now through repentance and obedience, the devastation and torment can continue to knock on the door of future generations. Many wonder why their children continue to make the same mistakes even after they, the parents, find Christ. It is the lie of the powerless gospel that has been spread, especially in the Western culture. What the church needs now isn't more converts. We need transformations. Transformations occur because of the power of the blood of Jesus Christ and produce a testimony. Most people still only have a salvation testimony. These are good, but I want to hear about what is doing in people's lives: today or last week or last month.

> They overcame him [the devil] because of the blood of the Lamb, and because of the word of their testimony. And they did not love their soul until death.
>
> *(Revelation 12:11)*

Transformational lifestyles are considered by the world to be legalistic. In our community and state, you are frowned upon if you don't drink alcohol or cuss.

The latest trend is even to ostracize you if you aren't supportive about marijuana, living together, or other relative truths. We are so intimidated by the possibility of offending someone, we water down the truth and give "seeker-friendly" messages. We must remember, that if we speak half-truths to bring them into church, we will generally have to speak half-truths to keep them there. Jesus is Lord; Jesus saves. Lord is who He is; saving is what He does. In the Bible, "Lord" is used thousands of times (hundreds of times in the New Testament alone) to describe God. "Savior" is used only a few dozen times in the whole Bible. What does He emphasize?

So transformation can be related to metamorphosis. A caterpillar is slow and very limited in its abilities. When most people come to Christ, they come to Him on their own terms. They limit His working in their lives. Then they wonder why they don't ever get off the branch of "despair" they have been on for a long time. Or maybe wonder why they are so attacked and tormented by so many "predators" of their pasts. Jesus didn't come to save us only. He came to save us from ourselves. We are called to come out of the world, not to be more entwined with it. We are empowered to be overcomers. To be new creations. To be set free! To go into *all* the world proclaiming and walking in the footsteps of our Lord and Savior. As followers of Christ, we are to soar with the eagles and not hang out with the turkeys in the barnyard. But when people begin to soar, the others try to bring them down. Transformation is neither popular nor wanted. People want a "Jesus" made in their image and placed in a box of their choosing. Scripture is clear that anyone preaching a different Jesus is to be accursed (Gal 1:8).

The butterfly can do so much more than the caterpillar. This is what happens when the Holy Spirit empowers you. He causes us to soar and see things from His perspective. We have been raised with Him (Eph 2:6). We are to daily die in order to be resurrected from the death of this world. Then we are also raised with Him in the heavenlies.

> *Those who wait on Jehovah shall renew*
> *their strength; they shall mount up with*
> *wings as eagles; they shall run, and not*
> *be weary; they shall walk and not faint.*
>
> *(Isaiah 40:31)*

Often people wonder why they can't see God at work in their lives. Maybe it could be because people don't wait upon the Lord. To me, to "wait" means to serve Him. Most Christians expect Jesus to wait upon us when we want. If the Lord is our all in all, then we can receive the promises encapsulated within this verse. If you want to be renewed, to be able to run and walk spiritually, then serve Him. To the level that you serve you can receive these promises. Some of you may be accusing me of preaching here about "works-based" salvation. Well, faith without works is dead. Scripture says that certain signs will follow those who believe (Mark 16:15–20). We don't chase after the works. The works follow those who are true believers. No one can earn their salvation. It is a gift from God. It wasn't free for Jesus; it cost Him His life. It's not free for us either; it will cost us our life and control. But we are commanded to work out our salvation with fear and trembling (Philippians 2:12).

I believe the only thing you can earn is promotion by the King. You can't earn salvation or His love. To whom much is given much is required (Luke 12:48). Remember the parable of the talents in Matthew 25:14–30. It's not how much you start with; it's how you invest it for the King. In the parable, the master allowed them to keep what they earned and even expanded the amounts.

God does not want us to settle for mediocre Christianity. He wants to multiply the fruit in our lives. But it takes obedience and hard work. Then if we are faithful in the little, He will give us much (Matthew 25:23). The fruit of the Spirit must be evident in all that we do too. Many great leaders and men of God have fallen due to promotion without humility and fruit. We must strive to empty ourselves, be filled with the Holy Spirit, and be open to the production of the fruit of the Spirit (Galatians 5:22-23).

The plant doesn't have to think about producing fruit. It just does it as a natural outcome of the right genetics, soil, nutrients, sunlight, and disease control. The fruit of the Spirit is the supernatural production of the same list. What do you allow to make up your lifestyle DNA? In what are you rooted in your life? What are you taking in through your natural and spiritual senses? Do you stay in the light of Jesus or continue to wander or dwell in darkness? What demonic strongholds or covenants have you made with the pestilence of this world? When I counsel people I boldly state that they are probably receiving at least some of the repercussions of their actions, and probably should receive more. Life may be fairer than we think!

You have heard it said before—insanity is doing the same thing over and over, expecting different results. The world, including the church, has become "insane" in its decision making. I have seen once living creatures raised from the dead. I have seen God heal stage 4 cancers. I have seen ears and eyes healed. I have seen legs grow longer. I have seen demons leave people. I have seen so much.

God stays true to His Word. He won't throw it to the dogs (Matthew 15:26). I have watched God heal the unbeliever or new believer on many occasions. Many times, when they backslide and run away from Him, the thing comes back and they aren't restored again. I know God is good. He can heal them. The same prayers go up in the same faith. Sometimes restoration and healings occur, sometimes not. This isn't judging if they are saved or not. It is only judging the outcome of actions.

I tell people not to leave a foothold for the devil. He is like a roaring lion seeking whom he can devour. He has come to steal, kill, and destroy, *and* is doing a fine job in the world and even the church.

So why have so many stayed as spiritual caterpillars and not transformed into spiritual butterflies?

Be Transformed, Become Obedient!

Why Not?!

Be Obedient,

Become

Empowered!

Why Not?!

Chapter 4

The Unwillingness to Cocoon

GOD'S KINGDOM IS NOT A DE-mocracy. It is more of a theocracy. Like Job, where were we when the Trinity created the heavens and the earth? What a great question to ask when we begin to bring God down to our level! He never asked us what truth was. He spoke it and now it is. We live in a democratic mindset, trying to make sense out of the King's rulership. In our rebellion, we think we know what is right. In other words, we continue to make "golden calves" to worship. What golden calf do you follow?

The caterpillar's flesh must "die" before it can become what God intended it to be. The gospel is very clear that there is only one way to the Father—Jesus Christ! It is His way or the highway! At the end of this life we can't sing, "I did it my way!" and get in to heaven. Not my way, but Yahweh!

Christians many times ask me what they can do and still go to heaven. *Wrong viewpoint!* They are still focusing on themselves and what this world is offering them. It should be, "What does Jesus want me to do?" Or, "What have I been empowered to do now that I'm a follower?" Notice I didn't use the word Christian. It has too many erroneous meanings in our culture. If we are true disciples, we follow Him. We shouldn't form Him around our life. We should form our life around Him. What do you do?

If we are bought with a price by Him, we no longer belong to ourselves. We no longer get to choose what we want or where we go. We are to be obedient to His vision and calling on our life. Now some people jump up in offense and mourn at this statement. They don't want to metamorphize. To them, not getting to do something in the world is God's restraining them into a "cocoon." Yet, the cocoon is the only way to become the butterfly. Therefore, most never become what God has for them.

God doesn't want His children stuck on a "branch" in life. He wants them to fly. But unlike the butterfly, we must make that choice. We must choose to allow His powerful grace not to just save us but to transform us into something beautiful and miraculous. The caterpillar doesn't get to see the miraculous work. The butterfly gets to experience it. That's what God wants to do—to work in and through us. But He must work in us before He can work through us!

In order for the caterpillar to be transformed, it must shut out the world by its cocoon. When we accept Christ through a life of following Him, we begin this process. I've said it before; it is not really biblical to "accept" Him. Jesus usually just said believe and follow Me! Then in the Great Commission He stated:

> *All authority is given to Me in Heaven*
> *and in earth. Therefore, go and teach*
> *all nations, baptizing them in the name*
> *of the Father and of the Son and of the*
> *Holy Spirit, teaching them to observe all*
> *things, whatever I commanded you. And,*
> *behold, I am with you all the days until*
> *the end of the world. Amen.*
>
> *(Matthew 28:18–20)*

> *Miraculous signs will follow to those*
> *believing these things: in My name they*
> *will cast out demons; they will speak*
> *new tongues; they will take up serpents;*
> *and if they drink any deadly thing, it*
> *will not hurt them. They will lay hands*
> *on the sick, and they will be well. Then*
> *indeed, after speaking to them, the Lord*
> *was taken up into Heaven, and sat on*
> *the right hand of God. And going out,*
> *they proclaimed everywhere, the Lord*
> *working with them and confirming the*

Word by miraculous signs following.
Amen.

(Mark 16:17–20)

The beauty of the butterfly is in its masterful colors. The colors we are to show come from living in the fruit of the Spirit. The evidence of a transformed life is shining through our love, joy, peace, longsuffering, kindness, goodness, faith, meekness, self-control; against such things there is no law (Galatians 5:22-23). To live fully within all the fruit will mean you will live above the consequences of God's law. When we break the law, there is a cost, a requirement that must be met. If we say we do not sin, we make Him a liar (1 John 1:10). We all sin and must live under grace, which empowers us to live above the requirements of the law.

God hasn't done away with the law. It is still His perfect will and personality. The Father didn't go through anger management classes when His Son came. The Father, Son, and Holy Spirit are the same yesterday, today, and forever (Malachi 3:6, Hebrews 13:8). Grace has provided a way to be able to keep the law, through God's heart. Our focus isn't on the law but the Lawgiver. Rules without relationship lead to rebellion. Relationship without rules leads to spoiled children always whining about their situations, complaining about why they don't have something. We live in a covenant with God. Every covenant comes with expectations and accountability. God's intent, forever, is to give us guidelines to empower us to stay in perfect relationship with Him. Most Western Christians and theologians still look at the law as a damper on what they want to do. Wrong! It is our tutor. Because we aren't perfected yet, we need God's Word to be our foundation upon who Jesus is, along with the Father and Holy Spirit.

We live in a culture of "victims." Everyone is a victim. All our issues are not ours and we blame them on someone else. Therefore "I" don't have to change! It's not my fault! Well, I would agree with you if you are Jesus. Yet last time I heard, He was at the right hand of the Father, interceding upon our behalf. So you still need to deal with that whole *sin* issue. Yes, we are not sinners any longer. We are saints who sometimes sin. As a result, take responsibility for your sin. Forgive others when they sin against you. And don't pick up offense for others.

It's time to cocoon into His image for our lives. Jesus wants and needs to transform us. It is then He can use us more effectively. In the everyday world, we see this transformation. We send our young people to get the training to be transformed into doctors, teachers, mechanics, farmers, nurses, and so on. It takes time and investing in their lives.

Jesus made the ultimate investment. He paid for it with His blood! We are not our own. This is why we will get glorified bodies. He paid for our old ones and has already promised these new ones. He gets to choose, not me! I am His to own. Yet, we still resist co-cooning (transformation). We have not made Him Lord of our lives, only Savior. Again, He is the Lord who does the saving. The captain of the ship determines the mission and role of the ship. Jesus the Lord determined to be the Savior of mankind.

We are so lawless in our attitudes that we see almost everything as legalistic. What used to be the "ditches" of lawlessness and legalism have been filled in by a perverse and defiling spirit. Holiness and obedience have been perverted into this whole legalism attitude that the church has redefined because of its covenant with the world. Yes, I said its covenant. Much of the church has become not only in the world but also of it. We have identified more with the world than the King in the kingdom.

We are going to look at some of the covenants people in the church are making with the idols of this world (demonic and paganistic) in upcoming chapters. I know this will not be welcomed by the world and many within the church. Yet, I feel we must rediscover the line God drew in the sand to separate His children from the schemes of the enemy and his destructive ten-dencies.

> *Each one is tempted by his lusts, being*
> *drawn away and seduced by them.*
> *Then when lust has conceived, it brings*

*forth sin. And sin, when it is fully
formed, brings forth death. Do not err,
my beloved brothers. Every good gift
and every perfect gift is from above
and comes down from the Father of
lights, with whom is no variableness
nor shadow of turning. Of His own will
He brought us forth with the Word of
truth, for us to be a certain first fruit of
His creatures. Therefore, my beloved
brothers, let every man be swift to hear,
slow to speak, slow to wrath. For the
wrath of man does not work out the
righteousness of God. Therefore, putting
aside all filthiness and overflowing of
evil, receive in meekness the implanted
Word, which is able to save your souls.
But become doers of the Word, and
not hearers only, deceiving your own
selves. For if anyone is a hearer of the
Word and not a doer, he is like a man
studying his natural face in a mirror.
For he studied himself and went his way,
and immediately he forgot what he was
like. But whoever looks into the perfect
Law of liberty and continues in it, he is
not a forgetful hearer, but a doer of the
work. This one shall be blessed in his
doing. If anyone thinks to be religious
among you, yet does not bridle his
tongue, but deceives his own heart, this
one's religion is vain. Pure religion and
undefiled before God and the Father is*

this, to visit orphans and widows in their afflictions, and to keep oneself unspotted from the world.

(James 1:14–27)

If sin didn't feel, look, hear, taste, or look "good" we wouldn't do it. We are each led astray by our own desires. In our culture, we have accepted a spirit of seduction. Men and women are being seduced into sin all the time. And not all of these are sexual temptations. We see a different "Jesus" being taught from our churches and the pulpits. We see new waves of doctrines being latched onto that don't line up with Scripture. Jesus was the Word of Truth that was brought forth to reveal the Father to us and release the Holy Spirit into us. In the beginning was the Word, and the Word was with God, and was God (John 1:1). This powerful Jesus was and is the Word. All Scripture is inspired by the Holy Spirit. Putting these two together solidifies the continuance of the Scripture from beginning to the end. We are to be doers of the Word. If you want the law of liberty, then be doers of the Word. We must also keep ourselves unspotted from the world.

Freedom and liberty aren't the opportunity to do what we want, but to do what we were designed to do by the One who freed us to walk in the liberty of being set free from the bondage of sin. The Christian who refuses to transform himself by having the Word written upon his heart makes about much sense as the caterpillar refusing to cocoon. It was designed to become a butterfly. In fact, caterpillars are considered to be "baby" butterflies. They are unable to reproduce until they become mature after the cocooning process. In Christianity, cocooning (spiritual maturation) occurs through the process of discipleship by the outpouring of the Holy Spirit.

> *We have not received the spirit of the world, but the Spirit from God, so that we might know the things that are freely given to us by God.*
>
> *(1Corinthians 2:12)*

God has abundantly given us everything we need to be more than conquerors (Romans 8:37). Obedience presses us into God and presses us away from the world. What pleases God is to walk in the Spirit. We must worship Him in Spirit and in truth.

So why don't we walk in abundance and overflowing empowerment?

Be Obedient, Become Empowered!

Why Not?!

Be Empowered,

Become Functional!

Why Not?!

Chapter 5

Obedience, Relationship,

Empowerment

I NEVER QUITE KNEW WHY WERE TOLD by God not to do something. I hear many people say that "God made the old covenant to set us up for failure." Or He "tried it" and then had to send Jesus to destroy it. Unlike so many others, I see the New Testament filled with as many or more commandments as the Old Testament. When we read through the old law, it was never meant to save us. Grace and mercy were already at work. Jesus was the "fully-fillment" of it. The law was never meant to save anyone. It could only point out our necessity for a Savior. Jesus has always been the Word. He cannot lie or bend the truth.

His heart is etched upon the pages of the Scriptures. It says that He inspired them. And at that time, only the Old Testament was available.

> *All Scripture is God-breathed, and is*
> *profitable for doctrine, for reproof,*
> *for correction, for instruction in*
> *righteousness.*
>
> *(2 Timothy 3:16)*

We can see the Scriptures are good for us. Yet He needed to cleanse the "temple," the body, so they could be written upon man's heart. His plan all along was to restore us to that right relationship again. Then we can walk and talk with Him. It took devout men and women in the Old Testament to be able to do this. Not perfect people, but broken and humble people. Now all of us can have those opportunities to come into His presence boldly (Ephesians 3:12).

Much of the Old Testament had to do with the outside. When Jesus came, He wanted to begin on the inside—the spirit and then the soul. He wants His Word to be written upon our hearts. In the Old Testament, the Temple (which was a shadow of what was to come) had three areas: the outer court, inner court and the Holy of Holies. The outer court was very unrestrictive in who could enter (i.e. believers and non-believers could be present). The inner court was reserved for what I would call the believers. The Holy of Holies could only be entered into by a single priest once a year after extensive rituals to purify the priest because God's presence who inhabit there. The Holy of Holies was separated from the inner court by a veil. The veil was torn between the two. They are one. But most choose to stay in the outer court. Anybody could go there. We are called to "come out of her" (the world) (Revelation 18:4), and to be set apart (holy). Instead, we choose to make the world another master.

> *Jesus knew their thoughts and said to them, every kingdom divided against itself is brought to desolation. And every city or house divided against itself shall not stand.*
>
> *(Matthew 12:25)*

> *If a house is divided against itself, that house cannot stand.*
>
> *(Mark 3:25)*

Is it any wonder people are collapsing inward? They are in and of the world. Although Jesus in us should be stronger, we leave a "foothold" for the devil to root in. We have become the "lawless" generation. Anything goes, including our holiness and obedience. Since when has disobedience ever been okay with God? We are talking about disobedience toward Himself. Again, obedience is an expression of my love for Him. Why do we question Him? If He said to do it, then do it! If He says not to do it, then stop it!

> *Whatever we ask, we receive from Him,*
> *because we keep His commandments*
> *and do those things that are pleasing in*
> *His sight. And this is His commandment,*
> *that we should believe on the name*
> *of His Son Jesus Christ, and love one*
> *another, as He gave us commandment.*
> *And he who keeps His commandment*
> *dwells in Him, and He in him. And by*
> *this we know that He abides in us, by the*
> *Spirit which He gave to us.*
>
> *(1 John 3:22–24)*

Jesus said He could only do what He saw the Father doing (John 5:19). Jesus was "full of the Spirit" (Luke 4:1). He denied His deity rights in order to become fully man, yet fully God. I don't get this. But I can just accept that He limited His power to rely upon His Father and the Spirit to lead and empower Him. This may be why He can now ask for us to deny ourselves, pick up our crosses, and follow Him. He was obedient unto death. Shouldn't we be too? This allowed Him to prove who He was and to set the example of how life should look.

> *God anointed Jesus of Nazareth with the Holy Spirit and with power, and He went about doing good, and healing all those who were oppressed by the Devil, for God was with Him.*
>
> *(Acts 10:38)*

We are to be obedient. We are to abide *in* Him! Then He abides in us. Then the fullness of the Spirit can inhabit us. *Then*, the body of Christ will once again be imitators of Christ. Nothing ruins bad theology or "stinkin' thinkin'" like a Jesus power encounter when a miracle, deliverance, healing, word of knowledge, or another spiritual gift rocks a person's life. We won't have to argue them into heaven. They will have just encountered "heaven" or the "kingdom of God" (Matthew 12:28). We are His instruments.

> *Truly, truly, I say to you, He who believes on Me, the works that I do he shall do also, and greater works than these he shall do, because I go to My Father.*
>
> *(John 14:12)*

49

We are many and have the same Holy Spirit within us as Jesus did. We must humble ourselves—our minds, wills, and emotions—before Him. We must be doing the will of the Father.

> *Not everyone who says to Me, Lord!*
> *Lord! shall enter the kingdom of*
> *Heaven, but he who does the will of My*
> *Father in Heaven.*
>
> *(Matthew 7:21)*

This scares so many because they don't spend the time chasing after our Father. They don't spend time getting to know who Jesus always has been. They don't spend the time submitting to the Holy Spirit's guidance. We currently have generations of believers that have come through the sixties, seventies, and beyond with rebellion and questioning authority. People know they are not right with God and yet get offended at the obedience issue.

As I matured in my walk, I have begun to see the relationship and love emitted through being obedient. I know what it feels like when my own children aim to please me. And I think that attitude comes right from our perfect Father in heaven.

Let no man deceive you with vain words,
for because of these things the wrath
of God comes upon the children of
disobedience.

(Ephesians 5:6)

We cannot earn our way to heaven. *But* as we gain knowledge of our identity is in Christ and who He created us to be, we begin to want to please Him by obeying every word that proceeds out of His mouth. Again, this is true worship, when our hearts, minds, and actions match up in word and in action with His. He has called us to be holy, to be righteous, to be a cut above the world. We have been set apart to be uniquely and wonderfully made in His image. We are not to look like the world and their father, the devil. Jesus will always be the prime example of how to do this. Then He taught that to His disciples and commanded them to pass it on everything that He has taught them.

So why can't we see supernatural experiences following the twenty-first century church? Why are we, as the church, a dysfunctional family? Why do we not see the signs and wonders that are to follow those whom believe?

Be Empowered, Become Functional!

Why Not?!

Be Functional,

Receive the Mind of

Christ!

Why Not?!

Chapter 6

Dysfunctional Living

When the strong man, fully armed,
guards his dwelling, his goods are in
peace.

(Luke 11.21)

WE ARE CALLED TO BE strong in the Lord. Then, when fully armed with the truth, our "goods are in peace." Our society and churches lack peace. We are a troubled society! There is very little peace or hope. People jump from fix to fix to find some relief. This could be in relationships, drugs, alcohol, money, power, education, titles, and so on. When we submit to

God, then we resist the devil and he will flee (James 4:7). We are also told that greater is He who lives in us than he who lives in the world (1 John 4:4). We must remember to be in Him; then He will be in us. We must remain under His "umbrella" of protection. We must remain out of the ditches He warns us about throughout Scripture (both New and Old Testaments).

As there is a promise in the above Scripture, we must also assume the opposite is true. If your family is not at peace and is being torn apart, then we can assume you haven't been fully armed. I have been under direction and instruction from the Holy Spirit and mentors on how to conduct spiritual warfare and the like. This is the area that most believers and even pastors don't want to talk about.

I have been involved in deliverance ministry for about twenty years or more, either as an apprentice or as my chief calling. There is nothing more revealing than to see a person who has been under the control or influence of evil being set free. Their whole being changes! It is also equally challenging to walk in spiritual discernment and realize the darkness and torment even believers are under after they come to Christ. It is a shame! Christ has allowed them to be set free, and whom the Son sets free is free indeed! (John 8:36). So why aren't they free? They lack transformation. We have taught the masses that just speaking a prayer, belonging to a church, getting confirmed, and the like are enough. There is nothing else. What a lie!

*The thief does not come except to steal
and to kill and to destroy. I have come
so that they might have life, and that
they might have it more abundantly.*

(John 10:10)

Jesus said He is the Good Shepherd, and the devil will try to sneak into the herd. I believe He is warning believers about how stealing, killing, and destroying will occur if we allow illegal entrance into our lives. To be in the herd means we follow Him. We listen to Him. We only go where He wants us to go and do what He commands us to do. When we wander into areas where He warns us not to go, the enemy will hammer us. Not because God chose it, but because we basically asked for it.

Let's look at some examples.

The first one is the demonic influence of tattoos. Tattoos are running crazy in the church today. We are told to not do it. Many say this is the old covenant and therefore has been done away with. But in my years of deliverance ministry, I see clear spiritual evidence of their demonic torment. There have been very few times I have not had to have the person receiving deliverance renounce their tattoo. The tattoos gave demons a legal right to be there and torment them.

When I read articles from tattoo schools, most refer

to the pagan practices themselves. In fact, a person I counseled (who is a tattoo artist) said he was taught to watch Facebook to see the depression of his clients. He knew when they would be coming in. He said it is an acceptable form of cutting. Not even one hundred years ago, these things were signs and symptoms of occultic practices. Yet we live in the era of accepting the doctrines of demons.

People are being tossed to and fro by every wind of doctrine. Jesus did not die for me to desecrate His sacrifice. He died to finally and permanently set me free. I will still sin, but I am supposed to be free of sin's power and destruction. Yet most Christians feel Jesus set us free from the law and its evil. It is apparent under the new covenant He will now write it upon our hearts. We are to obey every commandment He gave us. We wonder—or maybe you don't—why we are so much under the destructive power of a defeated enemy. It is because he seeks to devour who he can. We step into his snares when we are off the path of Jesus Christ.

There are a multitude of curses that occur because we dabble with sin and evil. Maybe we won't see much of it until our kids are destroyed because of our choices. Maybe our marriages will be destroyed. Maybe cancer or rare diseases or microbes will invade our bodies. All these things are running rampant and it's not because we are destroying rainforests or because of the climate change. Maybe it's because we live in and yearn for a "sinful climate" around us. We will be limited in our ability to grow in the Lord and walk in His anointing when we yoke ourselves with these and other cultic practices.

Tattoo parlors are full of pagan and demonic symbols. Maybe after we slide down the slippery slope some more, we will see more parlors that immerse themselves with "religious" stuff to legitimize the practice. We continue to see "tramp stamps" and the like destroying people. Again, in my deliverance ministry, it is common for the demons not to leave until the person repents and renounces the tattoos.

If you've ever been the recipient of deliverance, it can be intense. I have seen so many "new" deliverance techniques work well for minor or superficial demons. But they allow the real gatekeepers to continue to control and destroy. Rebellion is like the sin of witchcraft. These two aren't just related; they are one and the same. Tattoos have been used to identify violent and sexual deviant people. Police officers still identify tattoos with wrongful activity. Gangs and prostitutes saturate themselves to be identifiable. And the church wants to look just like them. Baal worship is alive and well in our churches today.

Some may think I am intolerable and judgmental in my analysis. I am tired of watching Christians flounder in their walk with God because of their evil covenants. Getting back to the tattoo artist I know and the training he was under, it makes sense. Most people make blood covenants with the pain of their pasts by getting these tattoos. They are covenants with that pain made with blood. No wonder we live in a society that can't get beyond their pasts. *And* more importantly, the church people can't either!

Under the covenant of Jesus Christ, we have been made new, the old has passed away, the new *has* come (2 Corinthians 5:17)! But not for most. They have made covenants with that pain. This does not mean they are not saved or not going to heaven. It mostly means they will live miserably while they are here on the earth. They will not fulfill their God-given assignments because of it. Consequences will be seen and unseen, realized and unrealized.

Piercings are no different. It is another form of blood-letting, another covenant we make with pain and evil. While tattoos are many times made on the body at "energy centers" from Hindu and other pagan practices, piercings are placed at the "gates" of our soul and spirit. They are many times found around the eyes, mouth, ears, nose, and throat. These are the entrances to people's insides; they are also the spiritual gates to people's spiritual lives.

We are commanded to taste and see the Lord is good. Hear Him. See His good works. His fragrance diffuses through us. His hands do good works. Yet again, we have placed gatekeepers (demonic spirits) at these locations. The result is that we don't use our spiritual senses to know God is good. We dedicate our downloading senses to hackers who want to eliminate any influx of God's goodness into our lives. These demonic spirits are the strongmen, the spiritual bouncers, controlling what goes in and even out of our lives. We can't take in the good, and we can't eliminate the bad. Poor diet, and no way to spiritually "poop" out our sinful garbage. Just like our bodies, we will become sick, even to death.

Other areas we see piercings are the belly button (believed in the New Age to be our life centers), genitalia (dedicating our children to pagan garbage), tongues (dedicating our tongues to evil), and so on. We are called to find life through Jesus Christ. We are commanded to dedicate our children to the Lord. We are commanded to speak life with our tongues, not death.

You may say you didn't go through a ritual when you had it done. But does that matter to the Evil One? If the practice is rooted in evil, then he owns it and has a right to torment you. He can only mimic what the Lord does. He has no fresh ideas of his own. Jesus said He stands at the door and knocks; so does the devil. We are commanded to give no foothold to the devil (Ephesians 4:27). This is a foothold! Our lives are like checkerboards; we can turn the board over to Jesus, but hold on to different squares of our past or torment. The "strongmen" continue to torment us there until we take it to the cross, repent, renounce, release, receive, and rise up. Then, and only then, will we become the new creations Jesus promised. Then we will know what "life and life abundant" really means.

The body of Christ has let another gatekeeper control the gates. Baal worship is alive and well in our culture and even churches: sexual deviancy, killing babies, prostituting our women, piercings, tattoos, cuttings, and so on. I believe we are in the last stage of the church in the America. There will be numerical growth in megachurches and death and demise of the small street corner church—then destruction. Churches will be museums as they are in Europe. People will scatter.

But then, a remnant will rise up! This remnant will not have desecrated the temple of the Most High. They will have stood apart, not getting as close as they could to the world. This remnant will have prepared themselves to endure, run the race, and fight the good fight. Repentance is the key to this revival remnant. They will choose to bow their knees to no other. They will be modern-day Nazirites, carrying the prophetic vision and moving in the apostolic power. The Lord will radiate His light upon them.

Many will flee from the intensity of that light. The light will hurt their sinful eyes and reveal their dark, cold hearts. Nowadays, evil can walk right into churches and almost sing along. We currently lack the reverence and fear of the Lord. Our churches contain more love (*eros* and *phileo*), but are vacant of the *agapē* love we are commanded to have through the power and grace of Jesus Christ.

It is time for the Spirit of the Lord to rest upon modern-day Elijahs to destroy the Baal worship and its prophets. Those of us that work in deliverance ministry and spiritual warfare see the spirit of Jezebel and Ahab running rampant in our churches and society. Control, witchcraft, and deception are destroying our people. We must rise up and separate ourselves from these practices. *It is time for more Mount Carmel experiences.* Whoever controlled Carmel controlled the spiritual life of the nation. This nation was God's chosen people.

We can compare it to the church. The church occupies a region. Then wickedness rises up. No longer do we worship Yahweh. The church instead gets involved in pagan worship—specifically a form of Baal worship. We go to the same mountain every week. We get the "feeling" and the pat on the back. Then we go on our way. All along we walk in the way of Baal. Witchcraft and deception run wild. Like Baal worship, lust of the eyes, lust of the flesh, and the pride of life are running our churches (1 John 2:16). Brokenness and repentance are absent from our vocabulary (definitely in our attitudes and actions).

We feel we can watch whatever we want because of grace. We can listen to whatever we want because of grace. We can have sex without being married because of grace. We can _____ because of grace. You fill in the blank. My dad always said most problems start at home. Dysfunctional choices make dysfunctional people. Alcoholics don't become that way by fleeing from the appearance of evil. As a regular bystander to dysfunctional families, I sometimes want to ask, "And you didn't see this one coming *why*?!" We worship on the mountain dedicated to "self-enhancement," and when we come up short, we wonder why.

Mount Carmel was a battle ground for control. Mount Sinai was God's mountain. Where do you plant your life and hope? Where does your family reside? Elijah went to destroy the works of evil. Then he went meet with God on Mount Sinai (God's mountain). Most people are living in the torment of Mount Carmel. We all need to live on Mount Sinai, and do battle on Mount Carmel. But we mostly battle with God on His mountain. And live in the midst of sin and paganism. We don't just live there, we partake of it. Yet, God knows our hearts. Repeatedly in Revelations chapter 2 and 3, Jesus says, "I know your works"! Your works flow out of your heart.

I will again say it; the spiritual mimics the physical, and vice versa. Do you still get offended easily? Do you still get bored at church or Bible study? Do you usually find yourself absent from church (locker room of the faithful, or full-of-faith)? Are you normally miserable? It's because you're still a baby sucking on the nipple of the Word. You still want the sweet, feel-good Christianity. It is time to move on to the meat of the Word—the stuff that's harder to digest, but keeps you full longer. It exponentially grows your muscle and strength. In fact, the amount of "lactose-intolerant" levels of spiritual "children" is growing very fast. Could this be because we are even less tolerant of even allowing the milk of the Word to taste good for us? So we find pre-digested milk for sale? I believe most believers never get to the milk of the Word. They are definitely too shallow for the meat! I feel the physical matches up very well with the spiritual.

A wise college professor once told my lab partner, "Two drowning rats can't save each other." This worked for the two of us as lab partners. But it also is for that person trying to find someone at the bar, or some other "depressional" palace. Birds of a feather flock together. Sin likes sin. Broken likes broken. People are looking for rebound relationships. Rebound jobs. Rebound whatever.

God's commandments, whether Old or New Testament, are best for us. Whether for societal or spiritual application, they are good for us! We must rightly divide the Word of Truth, studying to show ourselves approved (2 Timothy 2:15). In this verse, we see a worker does not need to be ashamed. So why are so many weighted with guilt and shame? Maybe we haven't studied and divided the Word of Truth. I believe guilt and shame will disappear, at least in the chronic sense.

We are double minded. We love the paganism of Mount Carmel, yet know we should be on Mount Sinai. A house divided cannot stand (Mark 3:25). A double-minded man is unstable in all his ways (James 1:8). Draw near to God, then He will draw near to you; cleanse your hearts, purify your hands—you double-minded person (James 4:8).

It is very clear that, if we begin to get confused, we need to run to Him. He will make our paths straight. A house or kingdom divided will not stand (Matthew 12:25). People don't want to hear truth! Truth magnifies the double-minded soul. When was the last time when you walked in a room the demons cried out?

I recently had a man in our church start a new job. He found out that God was in on this! God opened up many different doors to witness to people about life, suicide, drugs, alcohol, and so on. One woman in particular stood out but he had no opportunity to witness to her—just intercede in prayer. He got to work one day, and the lady came up to him and said that if he wanted spiritual warfare then he would get it. His "old man" would have been double-minded and flown out of there like a kite. The "new man," although a little scared, stood his ground. Then the Lord told him what to say and that was it.

God is good. He is pouring His Spirit upon all flesh. Praise God! He will finish the good work He's begun inside of us. This begins in our choices, flows over into our character, and overflows into our family. Although we only discussed a few areas of destructive choices, we know none of them are beyond Jesus's redemptive power.

So why do we hunger and thirst after this world, and not seek first His kingdom and His righteousness?

Be Functional, Receive the Mind of Christ!

Why Not?!

Have the Mind of

Christ,

Prepare for the

Lord's Presence!

Why Not?!

Chapter 7

Ushering in the Last Days

W E CAN THANK THE "NEO-grace" movement for the lawlessness of reinforcing the sin appetite of man. Why does the world have to change if the people in the church aren't even transformed? More than that, some teachers remove the concept of sin through the perversion of the "grace" movement. They teach that God tricked us in the Old Testament or He wanted to set the bar so high that we would be shamed into following Him.

The problem with society is the church. It is our role to bring the transforming power of the gospel to the world. But as the church loses its first love, becomes lukewarm, and is lead away by new winds of doctrine, we will see the Scripture in 2 Timothy 3:1–9 become evident:

> *Know this also, that in the last days*
> *grievous times will be at hand. For*
> *men will be self-lovers, money-*
> *lovers, boasters, proud, blasphemers,*
> *disobedient to parents, unthankful,*
> *unholy, without natural affection,*
> *unyielding, false accusers, without*
> *self-control, savage, despisers of good,*
> *traitors, reckless, puffed up, lovers of*
> *pleasure rather than lovers of God,*
> *having a form of godliness, but denying*
> *the power of it; even turn away from*
> *these. For of these are those who creep*
> *into houses and lead captive silly women*
> *loaded with sins, led away with different*
> *kinds of lusts, ever learning and never*
> *able to come to the full knowledge of*
> *the truth. But as Jannes and Jambres*
> *withstood Moses, so these also resist the*
> *truth, men of corrupt mind, reprobate*
> *concerning the faith. But they shall*
> *proceed no further. For their foolishness*
> *shall be plain to all, as theirs also*
> *became.*

The antidote for these last days is revealed in the last standing orders Christ gave us in Mark 16:15–20. Many downplay that validity of Mark's words because of their questionable origin. I personally feel they are viable and verifiable with other Scripture. *And*, these verses have been evident in my own life through signs and wonders.

> *He said to them, Go into all the world, proclaim the gospel to all the creation. He who believes and is baptized will be saved, but he who does not believe will be condemned. And miraculous signs will follow to those believing these things: in My name they will cast out demons; they will speak new tongues; they will take up serpents; and if they drink any deadly thing, it will not hurt them. They will lay hands on the sick, and they will be well. Then indeed, after speaking to them, the Lord was taken up into Heaven, and sat on the right hand of God. And going out, they proclaimed everywhere, the Lord working with them and confirming the Word by miraculous signs following. Amen.*

The key to these verses is that these signs *follow* those who believe. I have made this argument before but reiterate it again because of its vital need in the last days. We must have the same faith that the woman with issue of blood acted with. In Mark 5:25–34, we see a sick, plagued woman. Her passion just to touch Jesus caused the virtue or *dunamis* to flow out of Him, or really His garment! Jesus was so full of the Holy Spirit, it was even in His clothes. *Dunamis* means miraculous power. In these last days we will need His "dynamite" power following those who truly believe and are chasing after His kingdom and righteousness.

> *It shall be, in that day his burden shall*
> *be taken away from off your shoulder,*
> *and his yoke from off your neck, and the*
> *yoke shall be destroyed because of the*
> *anointing.*
>
> *(Isaiah 10:27)*

Although we see the word "anointing" here, some feel the best word should be "fat." As we feed our spirits by the Holy Spirit, they grow. A yoke goes around the neck of the cattle. Our spirit will grow to a point where it will burst the yoke placed upon it.

The last days have produced a climate where traditional evangelism techniques are found to be sterile. They no longer produce the spiritual reproductive results they once did. A culture of deception and witchcraft are ruling our country and around the world. In the USA, our leaders have spiritually submitted to these evil spirits. We also have watched our churches be led astray by the doctrines of demons for decades. No longer do we study to show ourselves approved as called for in 2 Timothy 2:15. No longer do we live by every word that proceeds out of the mouth of God called for in Matthew 4:4. Jesus is the Truth that sets us free. The Holy Spirit is the conduit of His power.

Addictions, perversities, and abominations are everywhere. Weather patterns follow the spiritual patterns of the world. Physical reproductive issues mimic the spiritual reproductive issues that especially Christians are experiencing. The earth is in the early birth pangs of earthquakes, and volcanic activity escalates. God is calling His church to give birth to the final great revival that ushers in the return of Jesus Christ. But He is first judging His church. He has begun separating the sheep from the goats from the wolves in sheep clothing. The list could go on. We are entering into and continuing on into the new Babylon.

This purification of His bride, the church, will allow her to focus on her returning Bridegroom. In the Old Testament, a bride went through up to a year-long process of washing and anointing with oils that would prepare her for the king.

I believe we are beginning the anointing of the church as His bride. But as Scripture states,

> *Zealously strive after the better gifts.*
> *And yet I show to you a more excellent*
> *way.*
>
> *(1 Corinthians 12:31)*

71

Follow after charity and desire
spiritual things, but rather that you may
prophesy.

(1 Corinthians 14:1)

When I compare these two Scriptures, I see the emphasis that we are to follow after Christ and look for the gifts to follow. Charity is love. Christ is love. Christ's love is the antidote for everything evil.

The word for "salvation" also means "deliverance." Many people feel they are "saved." But they haven't been delivered yet. We must be delivered from darkness, from the demons that belong to the devil himself. Being saved isn't a head decision. It's a heart change. Even more precisely, it's a heart transplant and putting on the mind of Christ.

So why do people shy away from God's presence and gifts in our lives for the church?

Have the Mind of Christ,

Prepare for the Lord's Presence!

Why Not?!

Bring the Lord's Presence, Flee from Evil!

Why Not!?

Chapter 8

Babylon Reborn

THANKS TO THE CHURCH AND its lack of truth, we have ushered in the new age of Babylon. Babylon was a key player in the ancient world and will be once again. Great speculation drives discussions on whether it is a real or spiritual Babylon. But to me, it doesn't matter. We will see its fingerprints across the globe.

> *On her forehead was a name written,*
> *MYSTERY, BABYLON THE GREAT,*
> *THE MOTHER OF HARLOTS AND*
> *OF THE ABOMINATIONS OF THE*
> *EARTH.*

> *(Revelation 17:5)*

In the previous chapter, we discussed the purification and anointing process of a bride awaiting her king. In the above verse we see a harlot. Much of the church has became a lover of the world, making her a harlot. We cannot love both the world and God. A house divided will not stand. This is why the church, especially in America, is probably in its last generation. I believe a remnant will come out her. But it will look much different. It will love what God loves and hate what God hates. It will be like the five wise virgins (Matthew 25) who prepared themselves with the extra oil (anointing) for their lights to shine in the darkness.

Many of the people in the church (and whole churches too) thought, if they would just recognize that Jesus is coming back, that is all that is needed. They had an anointing of oil for their lights to shine, but when it ran out, the current generation didn't know how to get more oil. That is my interpretation of the second set of five virgins. The current climate of the church in America is too much like the second set of virgins at best.

To be a virgin, one must abstain from the intimate act. Yet, as we have discussed, the church is dabbling with witchcraft, idolatry, and loving the world. Many worship the creation more than the Creator, much like the world. But the church just hides it better.

To understand Babylon, we need to have a history lesson of what it was and will be. Babylon is connected with the tower of Babel. Babel was a tower built during a time when all mankind spoke one language. After the flood, it didn't take mankind very long to rebel. In Genesis 11:4 we see:

> *And they said, Come, let us build us*
> *a city and a tower, and its top in the*
> *heavens. And let us make a name for*
> *ourselves, lest we be scattered upon the*
> *face of the whole earth.*

As with all rebellion, humans wanted to make their own name. That means they would have an identity all to themselves. It would be their way of getting to heaven. Because of their unity in being led away by their own desires to become like God, He scattered their language and the people. In fact, Babel relates to confusion. This is presumed to be in Nimrod's lands. Nimrod was a mighty hunter … of men! His name actually has a meaning correlating to "rebel." Nimrod was into astrology and magic (witchcraft). He was in love with himself.

In its day, Babylon was the political and financial center. Baal worship was at its core along with Asherah worship. Both were related to fertility. A direct connection can be made between these gods and "Mother Earth" and the creational worship of Wiccans (witchcraft and druids). Baal was the sun god and Asherah the moon goddess. Children were sacrificed to the gods as they passed through the fire. There were also piercings and tattoos associated and probably originating with this pagan worship. Sexual orgies and homosexual and bisexual practices were running rampant in these regions. Within the realm of worshipping the creation, we start to see the connection to drugs and alcohol.

As time goes on, we see king Ahab and queen Jezebel come on the scene. Queen Jezebel brought with her pagan worship, especially for Baal and Asherah. We see a weak, lazy man allowing his wife to be in control. On the other hand, she was evil. They had 450 prophets of Baal and 400 prophets of Asherah. God could not stand having His worship shared with these other gods. Elijah was sent to show God's power and authority.

Currently we see a war on men and their manhood. The spirit of Jezebel is alive and well in our country. We see a culture that blames the ills of society upon the males. We will continue to see the Jezebel spirit grow in power and authority in our churches, society, and government. And yes, this spirit can control both women and men!

Men are the vast majority involved in mass shootings, drug overdoses, incarcerations, and suicides, and they die much earlier than women. In fact, some current research shows that the concept of equal jobs and equal hours now favors women in their salaries. And we could go into ACT scores, elite college entrance percentages, grades, discipline referrals, and so on. Research even reflects that the majority of managerial positions are occupied by females.

Much of the current women's movement and societal trends are rooted in the spirit of Jezebel. Masculinity has become toxic. We have removed God's value and purpose of men. Men were designed to conquer and protect. Yet as society continues to degrade the value of men, we see this confused generation of men fulfilling these expectations, seeing men as rapists, warmongers, and angry, abusive, anti-women, and so on. We see the effects of a culture that is being manipulated by the Jezebel spirit. The Jezebel spirit wants men and masculinity destroyed, or least controlled. And it wants to see God's balance in the family and society shredded. It wants to be worshipped and to remove Abba, Father from our culture.

I'm not saying that men are perfect. They do evil too. What I am saying is that, as we destroy God's purpose and roles of men, we will continue to see atrocities continue to escalate. All people seem to live up or down to the value and respect we give them. It's time to quit playing gender warfare, or class warfare, or racial warfare. Our real enemy lies in the shadows and manipulates people to do its bidding. Remember, we war *not* against flesh and blood, but against rulers and principalities.

And yes, in the church there are equal but distinct roles for both genders. Both male and female are made in His image. Both are called to worship and into ministry. But we have left God's ordained balance and have chosen the social doctrine—one that is rooted in humanism and psychology. Therefore, the current "ideal" man has more feminine traits. God created them both, male and female. This gives distinctives and equal value of purpose. But not necessarily equal jobs or roles.

By studying the above history and current lessons being played out, we can see that Baal worship alive and well in our culture today. While we don't call it Baal worship, the rituals and symptoms are there. Imagine a pagan god who hasn't been around since Jesus's time now present in our land. As I write this, there is a proposal to build a monument dedicated to Baal in New York City in response to ISIS destroying Baal idols in Syria. Whether or not this ever happens, it stills shows me the spiritual recognition of Baal being alive and well today. Just think of it—a Baal monument showing its ugly head right at the core of America's and the world's economic center.

We see the spirit of Jezebel destroying the rightful structure of male leadership within the church and family structure. Blurred lines of gender identity are running out of control. The modernistic society we live in says truth is a false end or occurs in a fantasy atmosphere. We know there are no spiritual vacuums in our world. An absence of God's Spirit gives room for evil manipulation.

In Judges 3:7, the Israelites committed a crime before the Lord by worshipping Baal and Asherah. It burdens me to watch our society do the same as it allows the sacrifice of our children. In essence, we are worshipping youthfulness, convenience, and prosperity over family and life, not only through abortion, but through the lies of a sexually perverse generation. As sexual sins rise and become more perverse, we will see a rise in suicides and suicidal lifestyles as they increase in number and frequency. It's not about hate, but about loving God and His Truth that brings Life!

Our sexuality is at the heart of who we are and allows the spiritual attack of the enemy to have instant access into our identity. Torment and devastation will follow. The devil gains access through our lives by the legal rights of sin. It doesn't matter if you know it's sin or don't believe it, he will steal, kill, and destroy your family line.

Elijah was sent in his calling as a prophet. He was set apart to chase after God and thus was able to hear from Him. Although this was limited to a few people in the Old Testament, this calling has been expanded to every Christian in the New Testament. Most believers today are so wrapped up in the Babylon of today and the corresponding pagan worship that they have dulled their spiritual senses.

Once again God is sending the spirit of Elijah to destroy the Babylonian worship of Baal in America. Recall that 1 Corinthians 14:1 encourages us that prophecy is vital. Acts 2:17–18 states:

*It shall be in the last days, says God, I
will pour out of My Spirit upon all flesh.
And your sons and your daughters shall
prophesy, and your young men shall see
visions, and your old men shall dream
dreams.*

*In those days I will pour out My Spirit
upon My slaves and My slave women,
and they shall prophesy.*

It's going to take a new generation of prophets and
Nazirites to defeat the Baal society we live in. We are
also commanded to fast and pray. We have a church
culture controlled by the prince of the air, the kingdom of darkness, and the spiritual Babylon. Babylon
has been "born-again" more than we have. We have
been called to come out of her. Yet, more than ever, the
church embraces the world.

So what obstacles and idols stand in your way of
clearly seeing and hearing God in your life?

Bring the Lord's Presence, Flee from Evil!

Why Not!?

Pastor Wayne North

Flee from Evil,
Remain Pure and
Undefiled!

Why Not?!

Chapter 9

The Spirit of Witchcraft

Rebellion is as the sin of witchcraft, and
stubbornness is as iniquity and idol-
worship. Because you have rejected the
Word of Jehovah, He has also rejected
you from being king!

(1 Samuel 15:23)

THE CHURCH HAS BECOME RE-
bellious. We have left the righteousness
and holiness Christ commanded us to put
on. The "noise" of the world has drowned out the voice
of the Lord. No longer do His sheep hear His voice
and obey. We have turned our ears towards fables. We
have left sound doctrine. Lies and deception control the

landscape. We see a generation of men and women in the church that spends more time fighting in the virtual world than the spiritual one. No wonder we are losing the fight Jesus won.

The King has pronounced us to rule and reign. But we are being ruled over. We reject the Word of the Lord. God has never changed. He has always loved what He loves and hates what He hates. In the above Scripture, Samuel brought forth God's judgment over a king who was into rebellion and witchcraft. Yet Saul started off well. Are we any different? In short, our children will then receive a peasant's reward.

Witchcraft is present in just about every movie and video game we play. And do we think Jesus conquered witchcraft so we can play it more? Lie! We have a generation of brokenness that escapes into the fantasy realm. They feel empowered by the virtual world! We need to repent and get back to praying without ceasing.

I personally believe we have exchanged sound doctrine for "soulish" doctrine of convenience and compromise. The consequences of allowing witchcraft into our lives may not be immediately evident. Just like when sin entered the world, Adam and Eve didn't immediately die, at least physically. Those first generations lived on for almost a thousand years. Yet they were dead due to sin. We excuse sin by saying that, because we don't see immediate consequences, we must be okay.

I have watched a generation of adultery, fornication, drunkenness, harlotry, and so on excuse away their sins.

The emptiness is due to a lack of the fullness of Christ. It's because we are spiritually starving. I again believe we live in a world that continues to physically starve because we are spiritually starving. We, like Adam and Eve, want the fruit from the Tree of the Knowledge of Good and Evil, rather than from the Tree of Life! This holds true for especially the church. We aren't even eating from the right tree!

> *I beseech You, let the power of my Lord be great, according as You have spoken, saying, Jehovah is long-suffering, and of great mercy, forgiving iniquity and transgression, and by no means clearing the guilty, visiting the iniquity of the fathers upon the sons to the third and fourth generation. I beseech You, pardon the iniquity of this people according to the greatness of Your mercy, and as You have forgiven this people from Egypt even until now. And Jehovah said, I have pardoned according to your word. But truly, as I live, all the earth shall be filled with the glory of Jehovah. Because all those men who have seen My glory and My miracles which I did in Egypt and in the wilderness, and have tempted Me now these ten times, and have not listened to My voice, surely they shall not see the land which I swore to their*

> *fathers, neither shall any of them that*
> *provoked Me see it. But My servant*
> *Caleb, because he had another spirit*
> *with him, and has followed Me fully, I*
> *will bring him into the land into which*
> *he went. And his seed shall possess it.*
>
> *(Numbers 14:17–24)*

The curses of the parents will be passed down and realized in the generations that follow us. As with Caleb, it takes a different spirit to enter into the promised land God has for your family. Witchcraft controls us and brings curses upon us. There is a freedom in Christ to enter into His promises, which as a whole we are far from entering into in our church culture.

In fact, we see a church culture mesmerized by Eastern religion and New Age frills. We again have received grace in vain and have not just continued to sin but have expanded upon it. Our church culture has no problem mixing paganistic practices into their lifestyle because now we live under grace. Therefore, we allowed witchcraft into the house of the Lord, and even more importantly have desecrated the temple: our bodies. As I have said before, grace isn't the card that allows us to become more one with the world. It empowers us to say "No!" to the world and the practices it's involved in. And I really think in these last days, the devil will collect on any sin not forgiven under grace and repentance. Maybe it will come in your next generation having hard hearts towards the Lord. Or maybe infertility within your marriage. Or maybe drug and alcohol problems for your children. Witchcraft is alive and well in the twenty-first-century church. We have churches creating a spiritual cocktail of Christianity with just about any other religion we can muster—all because under grace God doesn't expect us to love Him by being obedient. It's time we cleanse ourselves and our churches from the filth of witchcraft and rebellion. It's time we show our love by being totally submitted and committed to His holiness and righteousness.

The final generation of the church will be instrumental in proclaiming the gospel like Jesus did and showed His disciples to do, and for us to carry on. In fact, as medications continue to fail, new diseases break out, pestilence consumes, money is worthless, and so on, God will move mightily through the obedient children. In fact, Revelation 2:20 speaks of a woman known as Jezebel who was wicked in the church. And because that church did not address this wickedness, God was going to judge her and those following her. I don't think it was just a woman named Jezebel, but probably also a spirit of Jezebel.

Witchcraft isn't just a physical thing; it brings spiritual garbage along with it. These two realms intersect, causing physical and spiritual sickness and disease. It's time for the church to become spiritually pure. We all sin but, as we repent, we are declared holy. We don't have time to be a harlot with the world.

What tempts you to have an affair with the world?

Flee from Evil, Remain Pure and Undefiled!

Why Not?!

Be Pure and Undefiled, Become Focused on Godliness!

Why Not?!

Chapter 10

The New and Improved

Tower of Babel

W E ARE TOLD THERE IS NOTH-
ing new under the sun, and the
Enemy's tactics remain the same.
He has come to steal, kill, and destroy. He also tends
to reuse tactics of old. Generally, he will never take a
Spirit-filled, on-fire believer head on. Usually he uses
temptation, distraction, fear, and deception to get believers sidetracked and separated from God's kingdom
purpose. Mankind has the sinful nature of always trying
to unify and to find honor to the point of even worshipping itself. Mankind has a submission problem to God.

We take after the father of lies, Lucifer, who thought:

> *I will go up to the heavens, I will exalt*
> *my throne above the stars of God;*
> *I will also sit on the mount of the*
> *congregation, in the sides of the north.*
> *I will go up above the heights of the*
> *clouds; I will be like the Most High.*
>
> *(Isaiah 14:13–14)*

We think we can be like God, and exalt ourselves to "godhood"! This is what happened at the Tower of Babel—self-exaltation of people in unity.

> *The whole earth was of one language*
> *and of one speech. And it happened,*
> *as they traveled from the east, they*
> *found a plain in the land of Shinar. And*
> *they lived there. And they said to one*
> *another, Come, let us make brick and*
> *burn them thoroughly. And they had*
> *brick for stone, and they had asphalt*
> *for mortar. And they said, Come, let us*
> *build us a city and a tower, and its top*
> *in the heavens. And let us make a name*
> *for ourselves, lest we be scattered upon*
> *the face of the whole earth. And Jehovah*
> *came down to see the city and the tower*
> *which the sons of Adam had built. And*

> *Jehovah said, Behold! The people is one*
> *and they all have one language. And*
> *this they begin to do. And now nothing*
> *which they have imagined to do will be*
> *restrained from them.*
>
> *(Genesis 11:1-6)*

Instead, of worshipping the great "I Am," they wanted to worship the great "We Are"! The city would represent the relationship to each other. The tower would represent the vertical exaltation of the "self" and the "us." It mimics the two great commandments:

> *Answering, he said, You shall love the*
> *Lord your God with all your heart, and*
> *with all your soul, and with all your*
> *strength, and with all your mind, and*
> *your neighbor as yourself.*
>
> *(Luke 10:27)*

The devil loves to mimic and mutate God's divine nature and providence. He does this through a false unity, a pseudo-gospel of secular humanism, and the degradation of God's deity to the commonality of a manlike image. More teaching and preaching, as well as movies, have been propagated in recent years portraying the Godhead as imitating mankind. We have lost the substance that He is God, and we are *not*! We will never attain deity. We will only attain what He gives us and ordains us to do. It is in Him and through Him that all things are possible. We can only do "greater" things than Him by allowing Him to do it through us within His power.

The power of the gospel rests in the death, burial, and resurrection of Jesus Christ. The blood sacrifice of Jesus brings salvation, redemption, and restoration. Yet, in the pseudo-gospel echoing through the walls of our churches, God is not angry at sin or He is not willing to judge the world for its sin. Repentance is not needed any longer. Jesus has already forgiven everyone from Billy Graham to Hitler. Salvation is that "free" gift that everyone has received. But it cost Jesus everything. It will cost you everything too.

We see a rise of an ecumenical movement that is rooted in "unity" rather than truth and substance, to the point that "any Jesus" is okay. This is wrapped in a powerless message of worldly love and non-transformational lifestyles. Therefore, we see a Christian universalism being propagated. There is no need for the power of the gospel to transform people through the sanctification process. And we see the its effects of this "gospel" upon our society. With the trends of sin, violence, and evil practices increasing, the only antidote is the power of the gospel preached through the real Jesus. Yet, the church wants unity at all costs.

The Tower of Babel is being re-formed in the

American church. There is a "city" of unity being re-built on the foundation of a "Jesus" made in our image. At the same time, there will be a real unity of believers being separated representing a remnant of the whole church. These will represent the "sheep" who hear the Shepherd's voice, obey His commandments, and do the will of the Father. The "goats" (Matthew 25:32) will be the larger group. Separated to their own desires of power and importance, they will seek to draw people to their teachings and thus build their own kingdoms.

The Tower of Babel seeks to control the verbiage and methods of man. They will have the new, and im-proved way of doing things. The simple gospel mes-sage and the power it brings won't be enough. People have to come to their "city" to get the updated version. We see this in groups that might have started off the right way but get off track in their applications. People flock to these "go-to places" to see God move. There is an urgency to find the place where God has chosen to show up. Then what generally happens is that they become an idol unto themselves. The people stay and they become a self-sustaining entity.

I do believe God has ordained specific people to lead, teach, train, equip, and then release people back into the place where people are called to root in and grow. God wants to move everywhere. We must re-member the temple curtain was ripped from the top down—not just to let people into God's presence, but to let God out! The church needs to let Him out of the box we have put Him in. I've observed more anointed people in smaller groups than I've seen in many of the "Mega-Wow" events. We are creatures of desiring bigger and better. But then we tend to overlook those who are God-anointed and instead focus upon man-recognized leaders. Mankind, including the church, likes the aspect of a bigger, taller tower to worship at and be unified around.

God wants us to unify us around the sacrifice of His Son, the truth of Scripture, and the transformational power of the Holy Spirit. We are called to do the following:

> *We are bound to give thanks always*
> *to God for you, brothers beloved of*
> *the Lord, because God has from the*
> *beginning chosen you to salvation*
> *through sanctification of the Spirit and*
> *belief of the truth, to which He called*
> *you by our gospel, to the obtaining*
> *of the glory of our Lord Jesus Christ.*
> *Therefore, my brothers, stand fast and*
> *hold the teachings which you have been*
> *taught, whether by word or by our letter.*
> *Now may our Lord Jesus Christ Himself,*
> *and God, even our Father, who has*
> *loved us and has given us everlasting*
> *consolation and good hope through*
> *grace, comfort your hearts and establish*

you in every good word and work.

(2 Thessalonians 2:13–17)

We are bound by the sanctification of the Spirit and the belief of truth given by the gospel. We are to obtain the glory of Jesus Christ and to be holy for He *is* holy. This is unity! All other "unity" is a partial or pseudo-unity based upon action or feelings of accomplishment. We are called to "*know* those who labor with us" (1 Thessalonians 5:12) which implies a deep "knowing" of each other.

We are to have nothing to do with those who know better and choose not to obey. This is hard to do when we don't know who we labor with. Blessed are those who are planted by the streams of living water. We need to be planted in Christ and in a local church body. It is here that our major ministry occurs. We do work with others around that group too. We have lost the heart to root into Christ and a local congregation.

So, what sins have defiled you that you need to repent of, and then let God restore you back to Himself?

Be Pure and Undefiled, Become Focused on

Godliness!

Why Not?!

Be Focused,

Choose Faithfulness!

Why Not?!

Chapter 11

The Ten Virgins

A S WE LOOK AT THE PARABLE of the ten virgins, we see that even those who try to keep themselves pure from the effects of the world might not make it.

> *Then shall the kingdom of Heaven*
> *be likened to ten virgins, who took*
> *their lamps and went out to meet the*
> *bridegroom. And five of them were*
> *wise, and five were foolish. The foolish*
> *ones took their lamps, but took no oil*
> *with them. But the wise took oil in their*
> *vessels with their lamps. While the*

bridegroom tarried, they all slumbered and slept. And at midnight there was a cry made, Behold, the bridegroom comes! Go out to meet him. Then all those virgins arose and trimmed their lamps. And the foolish said to the wise, Give us some of your oil, for our lamps have gone out. But the wise answered, saying, No, lest there be not enough for us and you. But rather go to those who sell, and buy for yourselves. And while they went to buy, the bridegroom came. And they who were ready went in with him to the marriage, and the door was shut. Afterwards the other virgins came also, saying, Lord, Lord, open to us. But he answered and said, Truly I say to you, I do not know you. Therefore watch, for you do not know either the day or the hour in which the Son of Man comes.

(Matthew 25:1–13)

So to me salvation is more than just stopping doing bad. Grace should cause that to happen. Salvation is more than just starting doing good. Grace should be doing that too! Salvation is also the expression of one's focus and intentions. No longer can we excuse ourselves by saying, "But God knows my heart!" Scripture states that out of the heart flows its intent (Luke 6:45). We are to produce fruit, good fruit, godly fruit! Any tree that does not produce good fruit will be cut down and thrown into the fire. But it seems that salvation is even more than bearing good fruit.

Salvation is also the focus of our future in Christ. The ten virgins were pure and were virgins by not being harlots with the world. But only the wise virgins had their eternal focus upon their readiness to encounter the groom. Maybe the unwise virgins were still more focused upon themselves than the groom coming.

A few years ago, God revealed to me that most in the church are, at best, preaching and teaching "self-help" truths. People love hearing how to become better or get better. But, the message of brokenness and total dependence upon the power and salvation of grace has been be replaced by the powerless "gospel" of "I can do it." Therefore, we don't seek godly brokenness or being totally and utterly dependent upon God.

The five wise virgins anticipated the groom, probably because their identity was wrapped up in who he was. All others placed at least some of their identity with the stuff they do in this world, and with this world.

The Lord has taught me that the more things change. the more He stays the same. He's the same yesterday, today and forever (Hebrews 3:8). Our focus and message in the church should be rooted upon this truth. Our churches should also be as founded upon the anticipation of His return as the five wise virgins were. But, our culture of church is focused on "me" or "us." People's "oil" is running out. Their once or twice a week attendance is not storing up enough oil to overcome the darkness of this world we see, especially in the last days. Our lamps should be glowing with the heart and mind of Christ. Not only do we separate ourselves from the world, but we separate ourselves to Jesus Christ. The five unwise virgins only separated 'from' the world, but not totally submitted 'to' God.

The oil also represents anointing in Scripture. I believe God wants to sustain our purpose until His Son's return. We are to walk in the anointing. We are to act in the anointing. As we seek His face, the anointing will show up. As we empty ourselves and die to ourselves, the anointing will fill the void left. God has prepared an oil reserve that is overflowing. We have not because we ask not. We are always saying something even when we are silent because actions speak too. Are you so full of yourself that you have no room for Jesus and His anointing? God is the not a condiment to add flavoring to our life. He is life. He is hope. He is just. He is!

The ten virgins set forth the standard of being pure and keeping ourselves holy. The other importance is our ability to seek Him with all our heart, soul, mind, and strength. Then it is promised that we will find Him. We will be in Him as He is in us. There will be no room for evil or sin. Yet we will still sin on this side of eternity.

But again, our aim is for perfection, because He is perfection. Only the five virgins who sought Him and prepared for Him to come, made it to the wedding feast.

Unfortunately, the church is full of "harlotry" having an affair with the world. It hasn't allowed the Holy Spirit to purify her and anoint her unto good works. Do we think we can go and do whatever we lust after, and make it to heaven when even half of the virgins didn't make it?

What are you seeking? Are you preparing for eternity or building your own kingdom? It's time for the church to begin living a radical Christianity needed for these radical times of sin. We have the only answer to all of the world's sins and problems. His name is Jesus! Yet we deny Him by our words, actions, and lifestyles. Like the five wise virgins, we need to make the Bridegroom (Jesus) our focus. Everything, it appears, prepared them for his return. Is the church doing that now? Or is it building its own kingdom?

So why do so many Christians settle for spiritual mediocrity?

Be Focused, Choose Faithfulness!

Why Not?!

Be Faithful,

Become Prepared

for Every Good

Work!

Why Not?!

Chapter 12

Preparing to Be a Wise Virgin

GOD CAN AND DOES RESTORE our purity and holiness. God created us to be holy and set apart. We were fearfully and wonderfully made in His image. Jesus said that He had to leave so the Helper could come. The Helper is the Holy Spirit, the One who empowered Jesus to do signs, wonders, and miraculous acts. Jesus basically said that He had to get out of the way so the Helper can equip us do even greater things. And if we are more than conquerors (Romans 8:37), it means He's prepared us to conquer and carry out His victory over the realm of darkness. He is looking for a bride who is pure and set apart.

First, in preparation for marriage, a king's bride-to-be would be separated from the commoners. We see God separating the darkness from the light. The future bride would then spend months being soaked in spices and perfumes to remove the stench of the world. This was not just covering or hiding the stench. Middle schoolers try to cover the stench by applying deodorant over the top of their sweatiness. Instead, they need a shower. We do too—a shower in the blood of Jesus that will turn every scarlet sin into areas white as snow. He wants to do the same in you. Are you ready? Or do you like shades of darkness in your life? Do you like the taste of sin in your life?

Second, the future bride had to study the ways of the king and kingdom. She learned the rules and her place. Her oneness with the king would empower her to help rule the kingdom. We, the church, are to rule with Christ, and carry the seal of the King. We carry the name of Jesus through the power of the Holy Spirit. Our weapons are not carnal. Shallow Christianity keeps the fight in the physical between flesh and blood. Mature Christianity fights the battle in the heavenlies. Which one are you? Unlike the sons of Sceva who were demolished by a demon during a deliverance because they were not followers of Christ (Acts 19:14), we'd better be followers of Christ. Otherwise this world will overcome us and leave us "naked" with no covering to protect us in this evil world.

Third, the bride had one real purpose—to focus upon the upcoming marriage. The five unwise virgins weren't totally relentless in their focus and pursuit of the bridegroom. Although they were much better prepared than the rest of the "church," they still fell short.

Proverbs 9:10 states that the fear of the Lord is the beginning of wisdom. Most in the church don't fear the Lord anymore. I believe a bride had a measure of fear, knowing her position and responsibilities. Her responsibilities centered around serving her king and his kingdom. Psalm 2:11 focuses upon a struggle she might have had of serving in fear and rejoicing with trembling. This is what most of the church in America gets wrong. Most are looking for a nice, palatable gospel that is focused upon a pseudo-love of the world. For a queen to do her job, she had to have a healthy fear. It is through this healthy fear we can truly rejoice.

The more we water down God's holiness and justice, the more we fall into a weakened gospel. This leads to the appearance of a "weak King" who is vulnerable and not respected by His servants. The church makes God into her likeness, rather than us transforming into His. We have watched generations fall to depression, suicide, drugs, alcohol, fears, idol worship, hopelessness, and so on. When we fail to see the true picture of the King, we will not respect or rejoice in Him. The modern church does not worship Him in spirit and in truth. They try to do it in flesh and feelings. Therefore, our lips say it, but our hearts are far from Him. In fact, fear and worship are two parts of a glue that fixes our eyes upon Jesus.

I believe that the five wise virgins loved what the groom loved, and hated what he hated. Maybe the unwise virgins forgot to love what he loved. They kept themselves from the world. But they forgot to seek a heart of love. We must refrain from evil, and to do good. We do this out of our love for Him, *agapē* love. First Corinthians 13 talks about this *agapē* love. This is love we receive from God, and must reciprocate toward Him before we can direct it toward others. At the very least, we can only have *agapē* love when we love what He loves and hate what He hates. In our actions, our focus is must be upon Him and not our righteousness. Man's heart is evil above all things. We cannot accept sinful lifestyles and habits and at the same time have *agapē* love. Jesus could only do what His Father was doing. He came to do His Father's will. God still loves what He always has loved and hates what He always has hated, Old or New Testaments. Otherwise He has changed, which is not possible.

But when we have our heart replacement, He gives us His heart. The powerless gospel is about rules and lists. The powerless gospel is about legalism and lawlessness. Thus, it's about us. What we can do, or not do, and still be "saved." The powerful gospel points to what can we do now that we are saved. The five wise virgins were preparing themselves to leave the world behind and to gain the kingdom of their Lord. They prepared themselves for the event!

So why do so many flee from the appearance of holiness and seek after evil?

Be Faithful, Become Prepared for Every Good

Work!

Why Not?!

Be Prepared,

Become Victorious!

Why Not?!

Chapter 13

Prepared for Victory

AS WE DISCUSSED IN THE PRE-vious chapter, we must be virgins, innocent to the things of this world. We must also be wise to the schemes of the enemy and the temptations of the world. Many times, these two areas speak to our defensive strategies. As a football coach, I know that, if my team spends most of its time on defense, we are probably going to lose the game. Defense is primarily a self-sustaining act. As humans, we have this desire to protect ourselves first.

A war is never won by retreating or flying the white flag. Like the armor of God, we not only are called to have defensive protection, we also are given offensive weapons like the Word, Jesus's name, anointing oil, prayer, and so on.

God did not leave us as orphans. We were grafted into the lineage of Christ. We have transferred our membership from a hellish ending to a heavenly reward. Our citizenship is not of this world. Our inheritance is out of this world. Our focus is upon the author and finisher of my faith—Jesus Christ. Our job is to run the race and finish well. Our commitment is to seek out God's kingdom and His righteousness.

So are we to be legalistic in our attitudes and behaviors? Definitely *not*! We are to be wise as serpents and as innocent as doves. We are to flee from even the appearance of evil and *not* to run to it. God designed us to live a life with minimal consequences of sin. Jesus suffered and died and then rose again to life so that we too can be more than conquerors through Christ. God designed Adam and Eve to rule over the garden and to subdue the earth. Instead, the earth and nature began to rule over mankind. Jesus took back the keys of authority. He has ordained us to be set apart to be holy, for He is Holy. His grace is more than just getting saved and having eternal life. Grace empowers us to live in Him and for Him. Grace empowers us to live out the Great Commission with the power and authority of His heavenly kingdom's mandates.

We are warned to not become entangled once again to the affairs of this world. We are called into action.

We are called to enlist. We are shown how to be strong in Him.

> *Be strong in the grace that is in Christ Jesus. And the things that you have heard from me among many witnesses, commit the same to faithful men who will be able to teach others also. Therefore endure hardness, as a good soldier of Jesus Christ. No one who wars tangles with the affairs of this life, that he may please him who chose him to be a soldier. And also if anyone competes, he is not crowned unless he competes lawfully.*
>
> *(2 Timothy 2:1–5)*

We are called to be soldiers. We are called to compete lawfully, and thus *not* lawlessly. Our flesh and sin desires make us weak and vulnerable. We dabble in the things of the world, even seeking them out. We justify looking like, smelling like, and imitating the world. Then we wonder why our kids, finances, marriages, and so on, are in shambles and despair. As soldiers, we are set apart for the desires of the King, our Commander in Chief.

Jehovah God is a sun and shield;
Jehovah will give grace and glory; no
good thing will He withhold from those
who walk uprightly.

(Psalm 84:11)

He doesn't want to withhold any good thing from His obedient children. Grace is the empowerment to receive what He has for us. It is up to us to walk uprightly empowered by grace to receive His gifts, unless we receive grace in vain.

By the grace of God, I am what I am,
and His grace which was toward me
has not been without fruit, but I labored
more abundantly than all of them; yet
not I, but the grace of God with me.

(1 Corinthians 15:10)

We are defined by His grace that empowers us to be His identity. His grace demands and empowers us to produce fruit. Just like it takes energy (sunlight) and carbon dioxide (along with other nutrients) to produce sugar stored in fruit, it takes the "Son's light" and the breath (Holy Spirit) to produce spiritual fruit. We must labor as Christ labored. This is true grace. Salvation is the first miracle of grace but its design was not to stop there. He wants to labor through us to produce fruit just as the Spirit of God did when He rested upon and within Christ. Maybe this gives you a new understanding of working out your salvation with fear and trembling (Philippians 2:12). Grace wants to labor in and through us to produce fruit just like a mother labors to produce the fruit of her relationship with her husband—a baby.

> *Working together, we also call on you*
> *not to receive the grace of God in vain.*
> *For He says, "In an acceptable time I*
> *heard you, and in a day of salvation,*
> *I helped you;" Behold, now is the*
> *accepted time. Behold, now is the day*
> *of salvation. We are in nothing giving*
> *cause of stumbling, in no way, so that*
> *the ministry may not be blamed, but in*
> *everything commending ourselves as*
> *God's servants, in much patience, in*
> *troubles, in emergencies, in distresses,*
> *in stripes, in imprisonments, in riots,*
> *in labors, in watchings, in fastings;*
> *in pureness, in knowledge, in long-*
> *suffering, in kindness, in the Holy*
> *Spirit, in love unfeigned, in the Word of*
> *Truth, in the power of God, through the*
> *weapons of righteousness on the right*
> *hand and on the left, through glory and*
> *dishonor, through evil report and good*
> *report; as deceivers and yet true; as*
> *unknown and yet well known; as dying*
> *and, behold, we live; as chastened and*

not killed; as sorrowful, yet always
rejoicing; as poor, yet making many
rich; as having nothing, yet possessing
all things.

(2 Corinthians 6:1-10)

Therefore, it appears we can receive the grace of God in vain. This means useless and empty. Grace demands a response. It demands a change. Grace transforms and empowers the believer. How much different would church services be if they weren't controlled and focused upon ourselves and our needs? The church would hate evil and love good just as God does. Our goal is to have no evil found in us, but we know we still sin and fall short. So grace must be invoked every day in our lives through the name of Jesus Christ. We must remember that we are just passing through this world. We shouldn't desire to look like her, act like her, or chase after her.

In previous chapters we saw what the influence and worship of Baal looked like and still does. We discussed the influence of the demonic realm in and upon the church and its members. And yet, the church is sterilized now more than ever. We no longer reproduce godliness and righteousness. We no longer make disciples made in Christ's image but rather in ours. We compare ourselves to other believers. Therefore, we become "good enough." If they dabble in the world, we can too! Grace empowers us to look to and act like Christ. Even in our failures and human frailty, the Spirit who empowered Jesus wants to empower us. He was and is perfect. We are in the process of purification through sanctification.

But most of the church still encourages people to add the "condiment" of Jesus to their life. In reality, Jesus needs to become life to us, and life more abundant. Scripture says to ask, seek, and knock (Matthew 7:7). We have not because we ask not (James 4:2). We don't seek Him out; we seek the pleasures of this world. He promises that we will find Him (Jeremiah 29:13). And when we seek Him, His kingdom, and His righteousness, everything we need will be added to us (Matthew 6:33). This includes the fruit of the Spirit for living a full life. Then we must knock. Keep pounding, focusing upon His presence and character.

My experience is that the majority of the church is not asking, seeking, and knocking. So this is why we are dormant and barren in the spiritual womb that is meant to reproduce God into the world around us. More likely, we are reproducing the attributes of the world and the demonic culture that surrounds us. We may be barren in the things of God, but fertile in the Ishmaels. Abraham became impatient in the forthcoming of God's promise child. So, he took things in his own hands and created an "Ismael." We follow the same mold by making things happen by our own might and power rather than by His Spirit!

Jesus came to destroy the works of the devil (1 John 3:8). Sin is the devil's door to steal, kill, and destroy in your life. But Christ came to give abundant life. What life are you living?

> *Do not be unequally yoked together with unbelievers; for what fellowship does righteousness have with lawlessness? And what partnership does light have with darkness? And what agreement does Christ have with Belial? Or what part does a believer have with an unbeliever? And what agreement does a temple of God have with idols? For you are the temple of the living God, as God has said, "I will dwell in them and walk among them; and I will be their God, and they shall be My people." Therefore come out from among them and be separated, says the Lord, and do not touch the unclean thing. And I will receive you and I will be a Father to you, and you shall be My sons and daughters, says the Lord Almighty.*
>
> *(2 Corinthians 6:14-18)*

In my experience, if we are not living victorious lives, it's probably because we are yoked to things we shouldn't be. A yoke binds you together with evil.

A yoke directs you and limits you. But when you are yoked to Christ, His yoke is easy and His burden is light (Matthew 11:30). If Christ is victory, then being yoked to Him is victory for us too. Without faith it is impossible to please God (Hebrews 11:6). And faith has substance. And a living faith in Jesus Christ is the victory, as the old hymn "Faith Is the Victory" states.

So, why do you keep your eyes focused upon the failures and even the attacks, and remain a victim?

Be Prepared, Become Victorious!

Why Not?!

Be Victorious in Overcoming the World through the Powerful Gospel!

Why Not?!

Chapter 14

Victims to Victory

WE ARE LIVING IN THE AGE of the "powerless church." Many Christians talk about God, at best drawing a cartoon representation of a "Jesus" that is palatable to the world around us. They have replaced His presence in their churches with an atmosphere of professionalism and entertainment. The gospel has become about man and not about God. They then have allowed the same demonic worship and worldly attributes into the church that Israel allowed into their worship, for which they were judged and led into captivity. And they think this new and perversely loving god will share his glory with any others. God said He is a jealous God.

The outcome of denying God's presence is to deny His power. We are need of His kingdom power. The atmosphere is saturated with demonic rulers and powers that are being summoned by the hearts and rituals of man. Our weapons are not carnal, but spiritual. Our faith is founded upon Jesus and fulfilled by His kingdom. When we deny His power, we deny His ability to wreck and ruin religiosity and the works of the enemy. Jesus never argued the kingdom principle; He came to reveal it.

> *Jesus answered them, I told you and you did not believe. The works that I do in My Father's name, they bear witness of Me.*
>
> *(John 10:25)*

The miraculous works that Jesus did speak of His mission and identification with the Father.

> *Truly, truly, I say to you, He who believes on Me, the works that I do he shall do also, and greater works than these he shall do, because I go to My Father. And whatever you may ask in My*

> name, that I will do, so that the Father
> may be glorified in the Son. If you ask
> anything in My name, I will do it.
>
> *(John 14:12–14)*

Christ said we will do greater works than He did. That is humbling and also a red flag to our current generation of lukewarm Christians. He's trying to get our attention here and give us the mission we are to continue. Instead, many are too busy keeping up with the neighbors and partaking in every ritual the pagan world has to offer. Sin has entered the gates of the church, and the masses are mesmerized by its appeal and our fleshly desires.

Then in the following verse He states that if we love Him we will keep His commandments. There are spiritual laws much like physical laws. When broken, these laws allow the enemy to steal, kill, and destroy in our lives and our generational line. God warns us throughout Scripture what He hates, and what He loves, what He wants us to do, and what He says not to do. The reason He is against things is not to keep us from having fun but to protect us from separating from Him, and to keep us from the attack of the evil one when these doors open.

It doesn't even matter if you understand these spiritual laws or not. God knows the cost of each choice. His love hates what evil does to His children. Maybe what you choose to do doesn't cause instant death, much like what Adam and Eve experienced. Maybe your choices don't immediately cause one of your limbs to fall off. But maybe your children will be disrespectful or hardhearted to the Lord.

We can't figure out all the options of the consequences of sin and disobedience. But I have experienced this in my ministry people with depression, anxiety, fear, loneliness, torment, divorce, addictions, cancers, miscarriages, deaths, and so much more. These are all rooted in the demonic even though they have emotional and physical connections too. I have watched, through repentance and restoration, God heal and redeem the situation. I have watched through salvation, healing, and deliverance the power of the gospel to reveal Christ, and ruin people's intellect and arguments against Jesus. Maybe it's time once again to let the gospel out of the box we've put it in and let it speak for itself.

Faith is the key to releasing God's power. Even a small amount of faith can move mountains. Putting your faith in Jesus Christ is about turning over control. No longer will you ask, "What can I do and still go to heaven?" Saving faith asks, "Now what can I do in the name of Jesus because I am going to heaven?" He opens the eyes and ears of your heart. You will be led by the Spirit and not by the flesh.

Faith knows that we war not against flesh and blood but against demonic forces (Ephesians 6:12). Faith focuses on Christ as our end all. Unbelief puts our "faith" in the things of this world, basically saying, "God is not enough!" This allows people to flee to evil, and not flee from even the appearance of evil. Some will still seek after the signs and wonders. They will be told to go away because Christ never knew them. But to those who chase after Christ, I believe signs, wonders, and miracles will follow their belief. Just like an apple tree doesn't need to remember what fruit it needs to reproduce, the DNA of Christ in the true believers will supernaturally reproduce Christ.

So what advice can I give you?

Seek Him with all of your heart, soul, mind, and strength. Flee from even the appearance of evil. Live a life rooted in prayer and fasting. Seek first His kingdom and His righteousness. Remove any appearance of evil in your life and repent of it. Expect that He can do far more than you could ever dream or imagine. Get rooted in a Bible preaching, Jesus seeking, Holy Spirit releasing, fruit of the Spirit revealing, gifts of the Spirit teaching church where there is fellowship, discipleship, and accountability, a church where evangelism is a natural outcome to a testimony rooted in a passion to follow Jesus Christ. And meet as much as possible with other believers to allow iron to sharpen iron (Proverbs 27:17). And last, hang around people already walking in their spiritual gifts and maturity so you can glean from them God's wisdom and anointing. And, … this list is not all-inclusive.

Please don't get me wrong! I am not trying to be legalistic, just biblical. God the Father didn't change because Jesus went to the cross. Everything He hated before He still does. Everything He has ever done has been fully immersed within His perfect love and righteousness. My personal testimony reveals His love and power that He wants to reveal to the world around us. Out of our worship for Him, He wants to empower us to take His beauty upon us and fly, much like the butterfly.

The world wants us to remain that slow, weak caterpillar. Our own desires keep us from cocooning and being transformed into His creation. His creative plan is to design us to finish well and fight the good fight. The prince of the air, the devil, and the powers of this world want to destroy us and our future generations. Yet, there is nothing new under the sun. The devil only mimics God's plan. He doesn't create any of his own ideas.

Thus, we are plummeting to the last days and final hours that will catch many in the church off guard. Doctrines of demons and itching ears will lead many astray. The new Babylon structure will try to kill the prophets of God and the anointing they carry. Not only do we need to remain pure and undefiled from the world, we must continually keep a watchful eye to the sky, looking for the symptoms of Jesus's return. He warns His church, prepares His people, and anoints ministries to break the yokes of bondage and to proclaim freedom to the captives. Jesus is the Truth that sets the captives free. He destroys every yoke of bondage.

We should be sick and tired of a culture impoverished in pain and victimization, especially within the church. The gospel should empower us in healing and deliverance. It should bring us closer to the mountain of God that will dwarf all other areas in our lives, good or bad! His spiritual gifts that are imparted to us will ruin the demonic chains as the anointing breaks the yoke (Isaiah 58:6; Isaiah 10:27).

The focus God gave me for this book is to concentrate on the chains holding the church and churches back from fulfilling His calling in these last days. The schemes of the enemy are not new. God's plan and equipment for executing His plan haven't changed either. We must invoke the name of Jesus throughout the earth—the name that causes every knee to bow and every tongue to confess that He is Lord. If we intend for our churches to once again flourish and overflow, we must once again invite His presence and lordship into our lives and churches.

It is time we don't just talk about our faith but show it. Don't just tell people about the gospel but let them experience it through the power of the Holy Spirit. It is time to let God out of the religious box we've put Him in within the constraints of our theology and traditions. I personally expect God to ruin people's nice religion and quaint Christianity everywhere I am asked to speak or teach. Letting God out of the box intimidates most people. Just as Israel backed away from the mountain when it began to move and shake in its signs (Exodus 20:18), most Christians have responded likewise. The closer we get to God, the more our sin is revealed. And most people don't really want to deal with it or change. The Light illuminates, while darkness conceals.

The key to the restoration of Jesus as the Head is to seek Him with all of our heart. Another key is for the church to restore His anointed positions found within the "Five-Fold" ministry in the churches referred to in Ephesians 4:11 to lead, guide and equip the church (people) for the ministering of the gospel delegated within the Great Commission. These "Five" ministries include the anointng of the apostle, prophet, evangelist, pastor and teacher. I believe this is still His heart, and thus my calling and passion. The restoration of holiness within our hearts and within the church will draw the heart and power of His presence back into the church. Then we will receive the revival needed for the church to once again flourish and reproduce the power of the gospel within the culture and world. We *should* expect God's *agapē* love to flow through the same methods of healings, miracles, deliverances, signs, and wonders. God's voice will once again jump off the pages of the Bible. God's presence in our lives and churches will draw sinners to conviction, repentance, and a new life in Christ. *And the best news*: This restoration of God's presence and power doesn't take years or decades to receive. It won't take dozens of books to read or surveys to take. God wants to ignite a fire of passion and revival in your heart and church *now*!

Maybe you don't get this or have never experienced the power of the Holy Spirit in the ways mentioned within this book. That doesn't change the truth! I was once told if you stand too close to a fire you could be burned, or worse catch on fire yourself. In this book's context, we should *want* to get close to the Fire (Holy Spirit) and be ignited by His presence and power. This is why I praise God for the men and women who are "on fire" for Him and for His kingdom to come and His will to be done—*today*! Their fire was contagious to me. That is my heart too! I want God's presence to be brought, revealed, and received wherever I go.

God's kingdom comes not just in word but also in miraculous power! And God placed His kingdom and eternity within me (Luke 17:21, Ecclesiastes 3:11). It's my privilege and honor to receive it, live it, and release it! As mentioned earlier, I have literally watched and participated in thousands of people receiving salvation through Jesus Christ, including those receiving deliverance from demonic bondages, healings, miracles, signs, and wonders. (Not done by me, but He who lives within me!) It grieves me to watch the absence of the gifts and callings within the churches, as well as the misuse and misdiagnosis of the gifts. No wonder the enemy is wreaking havoc upon and within the churches. No wonder the churches have been stagnant and barren in the gospel. We need to cry out to God as Hannah did for God to open up the "womb" of the churches to once again reproduce Christ. I've watched God do it in my life. He can do it in yours!

God has blessed me in working in the apostolic, prophetic, evangelistic ministries, as well as pastor and teacher. I have worked in many different giftings. I have discerned and identified others in their gifts and helped equip them and release them to be assets in their churches. Yet, I don't seek after the gifts, but the Gifter. You should too!

Prayer:

Lord, forgive me of my sins, my fears, and my failures.

Lord, forgive those who have hurt and caused me pain.

Lord, forgive me for just going to church rather than being the church.

Lord, forgive me for intentionally or accidentally partaking in paganism and idolatry, which you hate and for which your Son died and overcame at His resurrection, in order for me to live an abundant life of righteousness.

I invoke Jesus's name over every demonic force and spirit that has lied to me and encapsulated me in bondages of shame, guilt, condemnation, fears, unforgiveness, depression, failures, inferiority, worthlessness, confusion, victimization, poverty, pride, rebellion, paganism, legalism, lawlessness, and the like.

I ask for discernment for any other demonic or sinful areas of my life to be revealed.

In Jesus's name, I break off all chains of bondage and command all demonic activity to go to the dry place, remain there, and to not return to me nor hurt or affect any others.

Lord, restore Your ways and plans into my life.

I release You to rule and reign over every aspect of my life.

Change my heart and renew my mind.

Open my eyes and ears to your voice and methods.

Help me to empty me of myself, and fill me with your Spirit.

Let me see and hear spiritually.

Lead me, guide me, teach me, equip me, fulfill me, speak to me.

I desire to walk in your ways and be empowered in Your presence in the name of Jesus and the anointing of the Holy Spirit.

Break me and remake me.

Prepare me for these last days to know Your voice and to be obedient.

Empower me to walk in Your ways.

Help me to exercise Your fruit of the Spirit, and walk in Your gifts of the Spirit.

Help me recognize the gifts others have, and my need of those people to speak and release those gifts into my life.

Speak to me while I'm awake and while I sleep.

Thank you for not changing, that Your ways are good and perfect, and that You will never leave me nor turn Your back on me.

In Jesus name I pray, Amen!

Be Victorious in Overcoming the World through

the Powerful Gospel!

Why Not?!

About the Author

Author, Wayne North, resides in Wisconsin with his wife, six children and 2 grandchildren. Wayne has been working in ministry since 1992. He currently is the senior pastor of FREEDOM Community Church. His passion is for the church to regain its First love once again, and for it to become the righteous and purified bride of Christ. Wayne's mission is for the church to flow in the miraculous power of the Holy Ghost. Wayne believes it's time for the Church to walk in the foot-steps of Jesus Christ and to demonstrate the Kingdom principles as it brings the hope and transformational power of the Gospel to the dark world. His hope is that the Church would once again use the Biblical blueprint of the "Five Fold" (or "Four Fold" as some designate) ministry to equip and empower the people to do the ministry of the Gospel especially in the areas of the apostolic, prophetic and evangelistic. He enjoys seeing the power of the Holy Ghost bring salvation, healing, deliverance and other signs and wonders to transform people's lives and ruin nice religion for the comfort-able. Wayne's hobbies include coaching football, hunt-ing and fishing. His background as a science teacher and farmer have helped him make the Gospel real and relevant in his teachings and discipleship.

Also from Wayne North!

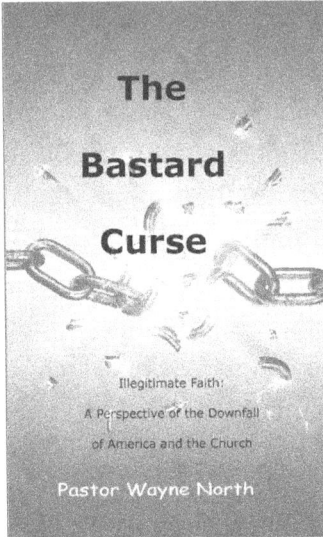

The

Bastard

Curse

Illegitimate Faith:
A Perspective of the Downfall
of America and the Church

Pastor Wayne North

We see dozens of churches close their doors each day. We must ask ourselves "WHY?" We see tens of thousands of people walk through the doors of churches, including the Mega churches, only to remain the same as they were before they came to Christ. We also must also ask ourselves "WHY?" As we are only evangelizing less than four percent of the U.S. population, we must ask ourselves "WHY?" We see the effects of only one percent of our culture that has a Biblical Worldview, indicating the churches are unhealthy, lethargic and even dying. In fact, many churches are DEAD spiritually even though they have thousands of members. Small or big, urban or rural, the churches have a form of godliness, but deny the power of the Gospel. Pastor Wayne North's new book The Bastard Curse examines both the "Why" and the "Why Not." It's a must read for all who take their Christianity seriously and grieve at the present state of our churches.

.

www.ingramcontent.com/pod-product-compliance
Lightning Source LLC
Chambersburg PA
CBHW060937040426
42445CB00011B/899